MAKE YOUR
CAREER
GO
BOOM!
NOT
BUST

**Practical tips to succeed
in an ever-changing world**

MICHAEL RYAN

ISBN-13: 978-1729501399

Library of Congress Control Number: 2018910619

Printed in the United States of America

Design by John Tamburino: www.itsjtaM.com

First edition, 2018

Published by: Ryan Media Consultants
Scottsdale, AZ/Gulf Breeze, FL

(602) 405-3140
www.makeyourcareergoboom.com

makeyourcareergoboom@gmail.com

DEDICATION

To my late mother, Cathryn Jane Ryan, whose unconditional love was a huge blessing in my life. Thanks to my sister, Sue, and her husband, Gary, for opening their home and giving her a great place to live in her final years. They are loving people. A special remembrance to my father, Thomas, my sister, Patricia, and my college roommate Steve Ragan, all who died much too young.

To my wife, Margaret, an incredible woman. God answered my prayers when he brought her into my life. She is an extremely giving person and has always been there for her family and for me. She has been a big supporter of this book and provided me with some excellent insights from her highly successful career in medical sales. I'm blessed to have her as not only my wife but as my best friend.

ACKNOWLEDGEMENTS

Thanks to the many people who inspired, advised and assisted me in writing *The BOOM! BOOM! Book* and now *Make Your Career Go BOOM! Not Bust.* Thanks also to those who shared their insights including Frank Broyles, Rita Davenport, Donna Davis, Dr. Sherry Hartnett, Jim Malvaso, Mike Mika, John Misner, Al Neuharth, Carol Perruso, Amir Raza, Tom Sadvary, Phil Tyler and Don Zrebiec. Finally, thanks to the people who graciously endorsed the book: Ken Blanchard, Jim Nantz, Rita Davenport and Joe Scarborough. All of these people helped me to achieve my long-desired goal: to write a book that might help others in their careers.

A few people deserve special mention:

o **Frank Cardon:** As you will learn, he was not only a great boss but became a trusted confidant. He helped edit this book and provided solid feedback. He has always been there for me and his and his wife's friendship have been a blessing.

- Sue Clark-Johnson: She provided me one of my biggest breaks, hiring me at *The Arizona Republic*. She ended up becoming someone who would provide me sage advice. She not only was a tremendous mentor for me, but for many whom she helped in her ultra-successful career. Sadly she passed away in 2015.
- Joe Scotto: A college classmate, he's not only an excellent golfer but a sharp editor. He's the one who came up with the BOOM! BOOM! theme. He also shared excellent career advice that you will read later.
- Ken Blanchard: A chance meeting on the golf course proved extremely fortunate for me. The legendary business author graciously showed interest in my book. He recommended taking my idea of revising and expanding my original book and creating a second book with a title that clearly tells readers its subject matter. For someone of his stature to help someone such as me shows why he's such a classy person.
- John Tamburino: An entrepreneur almost before he could spell the word, John started creating businesses at age 13. He is now a talented website designer and developer at www.itsjtaM.com

Finally, thanks to you for picking up this book. My hope is these 40 tips will help you succeed in your career.

TABLE OF CONTENTS

I. Introduction: 13

II. Starting Out: 19

III. The Road to Success: 59

IV. Taking Care of Yourself: 115

V. So You Want to Be a Manager: 139

VI. Taking Control: 161

VII. Finally: 199

CHAPTER 1
INTRODUCTION

PAY IT FORWARD

The conversations generally started around 5 p.m. Amir Raza, a bright young advertising sales supervisor half my age would come into my office at *The Arizona Republic*. He wanted advice on how to handle a certain situation, such as how to deal with a poor-performing employee or how best to communicate with his boss. As vice president and general manager of the Republic's 18 community newspapers, I enjoyed sharing advice and developing future leaders for the Gannett company.

Occasionally, Amir wanted to talk about life in the business world. He seemed eager to hear my perspective and the decisions I made in my career.

One of my most satisfying parts of my business career is the opportunity to help others – to mentor them. I was fortunate upon arriving in Rochester, N.Y. as a 22-year-old sports writer for the *Times-Union* to have Frank Cardon as my boss. He was almost twice my age and had prematurely white hair. He also had a quick wit and a needling sense of humor that he effectively used to get his point across. On deadline, while editing the last stories, he would exclaim, "just read it, don't memorize it."

Frank had tremendous people skills and knew how to motivate others. Some he would cajole, others he would privately provide feedback. He was the conductor and we were all members of his orchestra. A lot of my management style came from him.

Now, after decades in business, I want to share my advice – to help those starting out and those already in their careers. I've seen a lot – the good and the bad – and perhaps you can learn from my experiences. This is information you likely never learned in school but could prove valuable to your success.

My inspiration is like the theme of the movie that debuted in 2000 called *Pay It Forward*: That the gifts and talents we receive aren't meant to be kept, but to be shared.

That's the basis of *Make Your Career Go BOOM! Not Bust.* Why BOOM! and Bust? Because just like the stock and real estate markets, that can happen in your career if you're not careful. My goal is to provide practical tips so you can have a more satisfying, successful and Booming career.

There are 40 tips in all with a BOOM! BOOM! takeaway at the end of each tip. This book can be a resource not only today but as you progress in your career.

THE BOOM! BOOM! MOVEMENT

It all started thanks to Joe Scarborough. The host of MSNBC's *Morning Joe* and my former congressman while living in Florida was an early supporter of my first book, *The BOOM! BOOM! Book: Practical tips to make sure your career doesn't go BUST!* He graciously endorsed the book and asked his producer to schedule me on *Morning Joe* when the book came out.

My appearance on *Morning Joe* occurred in October of 2013 (the video is on my website www.makeyourcareergoboom.com). The interview sparked sales and interest in my book. Among those purchasing it was Dennis Slattery, a professor at Southern Oregon University. A few months later, after seeking feedback from people who bought the book from my Web site, I heard from Dennis. He liked the book so much that he started using it with his students to provide them with career advice.

That got me thinking: perhaps this was a market to pursue. While *BOOM! BOOM!* provides essential advice for people at any stage in their careers, it seemed especially suited for college students. So I began reaching out to other colleges and universities and to their professors and career counselors. Soon other universities throughout the country started using the book to provide their students a competitive edge in pursuing and then succeeding in their careers.

Big thanks go to Michael Wong and dean Christopher Callahan at the nationally recognized Walter Cronkite School of Journalism and Mass Communication at Arizona State University. Michael began using the book as his text for his class, After Cronkite, which prepares students for their careers after graduation. He also has me speak four times per year to his students.

Thanks to all the colleges, universities and businesses that used the book and/or had me come speak to their students or employees. That support helped me sell out of the first edition of BOOM! BOOM! and encouraged me to do this new book, *Make Your Career Go BOOM! Not Bust*, with even more tips to help people succeed in this ever-changing world. I'm grateful to all the people such as Ken Blanchard who encouraged me along the way. This book is my small way of Paying It Forward.

CHAPTER 2
STARTING OUT

Tip No. 1:

The Person You Have to Keep Happy in Your Life is YOU!

Rich Funke was a talented sportscaster in Rochester, N.Y. He was well established, well liked and well connected. In 1980, he got what seemed like a fantastic job opportunity, to move to Miami as the No. 2 sportscaster at WTVJ.

This seemed like a tremendous break for Rich. A chance:

- o   To leave the snow and gray skies of Western New York for the beaches and sunshine of South Florida.
- o   To cover the Miami Dolphins, at that time a premier NFL team.
- o   To work in a major television market.

Eleven months later, Rich returned. He didn't like Miami and preferred living and working in Rochester.

How strange? How weird?

Shortly after that, Van McKenzie called me about going to work as a sports copy editor at the *Atlanta Journal*. He was one of the top sports editors in the country. Pam Armstrong Hunt, my first boss in Binghamton, N.Y. after college in 1977, had recommended me. By then she had moved to Atlanta and I had moved on to Rochester and was sports editor of the *Times-Union*.

I loved my job and living in Rochester but Van McKenzie was a legend in the newspaper sports business. He wanted to make the *Atlanta Journal* one of the premier sports sections in the country and was building the team to do that. He wanted me to join his team.

The *Journal* flew me down for a whirlwind visit to Atlanta. The people seemed great, and working in a major sports market was appealing. Van offered me a job and then said, "You come here and by age 30 you will be a sports editor at a major newspaper in the country."

My head was spinning. I raced back to the airport, almost missing my flight – the gate attendant ended up putting me in first class – and hurried home to play softball that night. The trip seemed almost surreal.

After turning down many job offers over the previous 18 months, I thought, "How can I turn down this one? I'm 25 years old, I shouldn't be that content with my job and my life."

Van called a day later and wanted my answer. I asked for more money and an extra week before starting. He agreed and then said, "You are planning to come?"

I felt boxed in. As a colleague said, "If you've asked for more money and he's given it to you, you're pretty much obligated to take the job."

The next three weeks were grueling – packing and getting ready to leave my friends, a job I loved and what seemed like my life.

Every time my roommate, Steve Ragan, and I would go out, whether to a bar or simply to eat, he would say, "This will be the last time you'll ever be here."

Three days before my scheduled start in Atlanta, I made the two-hour drive from Rochester to my parents' home in Elmira, N.Y. That night, a friend, Mark Murphy, and I went to play tennis. I could hardly play. I was so bummed out. I felt my life was ending at age 25.

The next day, I got up and sadly said goodbye to my parents. It was going to take two full days to drive to Atlanta. My plan was to drive halfway and spend the first night in Salem, Va.

That was the longest day of my life. I remember driving along so depressed. This was before cell phones so there was no one to talk with along the way. I felt like I had thrown my life away. Hour after hour of being alone in a car can drive you crazy.

That night I ended up staying at a Sheraton Inn. I went down to the restaurant to eat but hardly touched my meal.

The next morning, I got up and went to Mass before hitting the road. I felt so alone and so distraught. After Mass, I went to see the priest. We talked for about a half an hour. He helped me sort through my feelings. Afterward, I decided I wanted to go back to Rochester. I called my boss, Frank Cardon, the executive sports editor. Like the prodigal son, he and the editor, Bob Giles, welcomed me back.

I had to call Van McKenzie and tell him that I wasn't coming to Atlanta. I had to call the movers and tell them to send my stuff back to Rochester.

I had made my decision to go to Atlanta not because that's what I wanted, but because that's what other people thought was best for me. At the time, I didn't care about being a sports editor at a major newspaper by the time I was 30. I was happy where I was.

That's when I began to understand better Rich Funke's decision. I had been thinking he was crazy to leave Miami to return to Rochester because that's what I thought was best for him. Not what he thought was best for him.

The lesson out of my Atlanta experience is this: The person in life you have to keep happy is yourself.

Too often people in life make decisions – where to go to college, what to do for a profession, where to live – based on what other people think. But remember, they aren't the ones who have to go to that college, do that job or live in a certain area – you are. People will always have plenty of ideas on what you should do because it's easier to give advice than to take advice.

As for Rich Funke, he ended up having a distinguished career in television in Rochester, first as sports anchor and then as the primary nightly news anchor.

He ended up retiring from television and was inducted into the New York State Broadcasters Association Hall of Fame with Mike Wallace and Len Berman in 2012. He now is a New York state senator.

Two final notes about Atlanta:

1. If you're ever going to make a move, take a friend along for the ride. In any emotional or life-changing situation, it's much easier if you have support. A person I mentor actually applied that lesson by taking someone along when he drove from Phoenix to Houston to start a new job in an unfamiliar city.

2. It all worked out. Shortly after returning, I met the woman who would be my wife and I can't imagine spending my life with anyone else.

BOOM! BOOM!

Remember you are in charge of your career. It's great to listen to advice but you are the one who has to do the job.

Tip No. 2:

Who's Driving Your Car?

Imagine that your career is like a car. Where are you sitting in that car?

Are you:

- o **In the driver's seat,** firmly holding on to the steering wheel?
- o **In the passenger's seat,** watching as the driver is in control?
- o **In the back seat,** looking out the window watching the world go by?
- o **In the trunk,** stuffed in along with everything else?

The answer is obvious: you need to be in the driver's seat.

Sadly, too many people aren't driving their career car. They're letting other people and other situations drive it for them.

Remember: the person who should care the most about your career is YOU!

Why would you let others take control of your career?

Being in the driver's seat means being in charge. It means being proactive and not passive about your career.

What does that mean? Too many people sit back and don't develop a plan for their career. They look to others to chart their course. They expect others – such as bosses – to present opportunities to them.

That's not smart. Other people might not know exactly what you want in your career.

As I like to say, a lot of people have ESPN, they don't have ESP. People won't know what you want unless you tell them.

When looking for a job or a promotion, reach out to people and let them know what you desire. Ask if they can help. What's the worst thing they can say: No? Then, if they can't help, ask if they know anyone who might be able to help.

If you don't ask, you're likely not going to get what you want. There are people out there who could help if you only ask.

A friend was looking to switch careers and do something different. She didn't sit back and just hope something would happen. She reached out to her contacts, told them what she desired, and asked if they knew anyone at the company she wanted to join.

One of her contacts knew somebody at that company. That person arranged a meeting for her. She ended up getting hired and is much happier.

This woman knew she was in the driver's seat of her career.

There are many great resources out there of people potentially willing to help. LinkedIn allows you to see who you know and who others know. Also, reach out to alumni from your college or university. There is a bond among people who attended the same place. Alumni often are willing to assist if only asked.

A fisherman knows to catch a lot of fish, he or she needs to cast a wide net. The same is true when looking for a job. The more people who know what you want, the more people there are who can possibly help you.

BOOM! BOOM!

Where are you in your career car? Make sure you are sitting comfortably in the driver's seat, steering your way through all the curves and straightaways.

Tip No. 3:

Monday vs. Friday People

This sounds so simple but yet so true. There really are two types of people in the world: Monday people and Friday people.

What could that possibly mean?

Monday people are those who look forward to going back to work and don't dread that the weekend is over. They enjoy their jobs and find satisfaction in them. Friday people are those who spend all week counting down to Friday night and the start of another weekend. They see work as a necessary evil that they do to have money for the weekend.

Not surprising, Monday people are more successful in their careers.

Why is this important? Do the math? Most people work five out of a seven-day week. That means they are working 71.4% of the week as opposed to being off 28.6% of the week. If you don't enjoy your work, that means you could be miserable almost

---

three quarters of your life.

That's why it is important to find a career that you enjoy and a job that you find satisfying and rewarding.

Fortunately I found satisfaction in my career.

However, I wasn't so sure of that when my full-time career started.

I remember my final semester at St. Bonaventure University in Olean, N.Y. It was time to look for a job after graduation. I had received a Newspaper Fund scholarship the previous summer and had interned in Rochester. A former Newspaper Fund intern who was then copy desk chief at the *Binghamton* (N.Y.) *Sun-Bulletin* called and wanted to interview me for a copy editing position.

I went to the interview and was offered the job in March. At that time, graduation seemed far off. Senior year was a blast and I didn't want to believe that my college years would soon end. When my new employers wanted a start date, I agreed to begin three days after graduation. Unrealistically I kept thinking that graduation would never come, so that meant three days after graduation would never come.

Reality bites.

I remember driving on graduation morning to pick up my parents at the hotel. I had only slept a couple hours and in my fog it finally dawned on me: "I'm graduating today."

Sure enough. Three days later came and I was in the newsroom of the *Binghamton Sun-Bulletin*.

Then it hit me: "I've got to do this for the next 44 years." In previous jobs, I always knew that it wasn't permanent and that I would soon head back to college. Now that wasn't an option. I had joined the working world.

That's why it is so important to find a job that you care passionately about; a job that keeps you motivated and brings you much satisfaction. Too often, people get hung up on how much the job pays or the benefits.

One of the saddest things is seeing people who hate their jobs but do them because of the money or because they feel stuck.

There's a friend who used to get physically sick on Sunday nights because he dreaded that the weekend was over and he had to go back to work. On the surface, people would have thought he was extremely successful because he had a prestigious job, making great money and working for a highly respected company. He just hated what he was doing. He eventually had to resign his job because it so impacted his health.

Don't get caught in that same trap.

The late Apple founder Steve Jobs said it best during his commencement speech at Stanford University:

"When I was 17, I read a quote that went something like: 'If you live each day as if it was your last, someday you'll most certainly be right.' It made an impression on me, and since then, for the past 33 years, I have looked in the mirror every morning and asked myself: 'If today were the last day of my life, would I want to do what I am about to do today?' And whenever the answer has been 'No' for too many days in a row, I know I need to change something."

BOOM! BOOM!

Since you will likely work for the longest part of your life, find a job that you enjoy. Be a Monday person, not a Friday person. Otherwise it could be one long, lousy life.

Tip No. 4:

Your Career is Like Building a House

One of my favorite analogies when talking with young people about their careers is to encourage them to think of their career as a house.

The most important part of building a house is putting in a strong and sturdy foundation. Once the foundation is secure, then the builder can frame the walls, put the roof on, install windows, put the siding on, do the electrical and plumbing work, hang the drywall, install the floor and do the finish work.

Too often young people are in such a rush to advance their careers that like an inexperienced home builder they skimp on the foundation and start putting up the walls and the roof. They don't spend the time learning their craft and gaining the necessary skills to succeed long term.

Having a slipshod foundation might not matter when times are good, but watch out when storms hit. As someone who has lived through many hurricanes, houses crumble if the foundation isn't well fortified.

The same is true with careers.

Some people get promoted who aren't prepared for their new jobs. Frequently it catches up with them. They never fully develop the skills they need to succeed. When their careers plateau, they become frustrated and some leave the business.

Don't let that happen to you. Take the time to build a strong foundation. Here are some ideas:

- o Make sure you understand the core essentials of your business.
- o Learn as much as you can about your job and the jobs you would like to have going forward.
- o Seek out people who do well in the same job that you hold and find out what makes them successful.
- o Seek out a mentor who cares about you and can provide insights and act as a sounding board for you.
- o Volunteer to take on additional assignments especially those that give you experience in other facets of the business.
- o Continue to sharpen your skills and realize the skills you have today might not be all the ones you need to succeed in the future.

One of Aesop's most famous fables involves a tortoise and a hare. The hare mocks the tortoise and challenges him to a race. The hare starts out fast then, because he's so cocky, takes a nap along the way. When he finally awakes and gets going, the tortoise beats him to the finish line.

You don't want to end up like that hare – starting strong but then not spending the necessary time getting the experience and training that will help you succeed in the end.

Remember, today's hotshot can easily become tomorrow's forgotten person.

Make sure your career isn't like a piece of furniture with a shiny veneer finish. When you look closely, underneath that veneer is just particle board.

BOOM! BOOM!

Take the time in your career to build a solid foundation. As a marathon runner knows, the race isn't won after the first mile. The same goes for your career.

Tip No. 5:

Work is Like School:
You're Only Graded on Performance

Remember that person in college who spent 20 hours studying for an exam only to end up with a C for a grade. Then remember that person who spent only two hours studying and got an A.

How fair is that? Well, that's life.

We're not graded on the number of hours we put into studying for a test or working on a project. We're graded on the results.

That's why it is important to spend your time wisely. Too often people are studying material that is not relevant or working on parts of a project that aren't going to produce results.

People think they are studying hard when they know they're not. They're jumping around the library, visiting with others. Or they're sitting in their room, supposedly studying with the stereo blaring and friends walking in and out. They're putting in non-productive hours.

The same is true for careers. Sometimes people think they are working hard, but they're really not. They're distracted. They're not focused. Then they are bummed when "all their hours of work" don't produce results.

One of my favorite quotes comes from Frank Broyles, legendary football coach at the University of Arkansas. When he retired as coach in 1984 to become full- time athletic director, he hired Ken Hatfield, a former player of his at Arkansas, to succeed him. Hatfield had been coaching at the Air Force Academy.

After Hatfield went 7-4-1 in his first season, someone asked Frank Broyles if he would still like Ken Hatfield if he had had a losing season.

"Like 'em, sure I'd like 'em," said Broyles, in his Southern drawl. "And I'd miss 'em, too."

Fortunately for Hatfield, he went 10-2 the next season and ended up his Arkansas career with a 55-17-1 record.

The moral of the story: If you don't produce results, no matter how well you are liked, you're probably not going to keep your job.

This is especially true in sales. It's a results-oriented profession.

Either you make your number or you don't. If you keep missing your number, you're likely going to lose your job. You can have plenty of reasons for not succeeding – bad economy, lousy territory, inferior product – but in the end you didn't make goal.

Just like a football owner will fire a coach for not winning, so will a boss – no matter how much he or she likes the person.

Being well liked is not necessarily a recipe for success. A person can be difficult to manage, but if he or she consistently exceeds goal, an organization will likely keep that person. Management will put up with that person's complaining.

But watch out if that person stops making goal. That person will be out the door faster than a New York fashion model can change clothes.

Businesses often will put up with a successful pain in the butt. They won't put up with a failing pain in the butt.

BOOM! BOOM!

As blunt-talking sports host Jim Rome says, "Scoreboard, baby." In the end, the results are what matters.

Tip No. 6:

The Distinction Between Bitching and a Fundamental Difference

---

At age 22, two years after interning at the *Times-Union*, I returned as a sports writer/sports copy editor. This was a big deal to me since Rochester was the home of Gannett, the nation's largest newspaper company, and the T-U was one of its best newspapers.

I replaced Carol Perruso, who left to join the *San Diego Union-Tribune*. About a year later, a colleague of mine, Bill Koenig, and I had lunch with her while visiting California.

Carol offered some profound advice: "Know the Distinction Between Bitching and a Fundamental Difference."
In any job, she said, there's going to be bitching. You are overworked, there are not enough resources, there's not enough time. You might as well accept that. The real issue is if you have a fundamental or philosophical difference with the way the company is being run. Then you have two choices: accept it or leave. It's that simple.

People often wander from job to job thinking there's some perfect job out there. Then they become disappointed when they realize they are experiencing the same frustrations – sometimes worse – than they experienced in a previous job. Instead of realizing that that comes with the job, they just keep moving on.

The time to move on is when you have a fundamental difference with the company. You might not like their short- or long-term plan. You might not like the character of the people or the ethics of top management. You're likely not going to change them. It's you who has to change. It's time to leave.

Recently, Carol and I talked. She had gone on from San Diego to the *Los Angeles Times* where she worked for 20 years, the last 2 ½ years as president of *LATimes.com*.

Here's her addendum to what she shared with me back then and what she shared with her staff when she left the *Times*.
"If one of the criteria in a job is not having fun, then there are plenty of jobs out there," she said. "So you've got to look for a job that has fun. That's always been my philosophy."

One of the most amazing truths about business: happy, contented people in their jobs are often the ones to get recruited by other companies; whiners simply stay and whine.

At age 25, shortly after becoming sports editor in Rochester, I received job offers from many newspapers throughout the country. This was because promising young sports editors were tougher to find than talented young sports writers.

I was extremely happy in Rochester. I loved my job, my colleagues, my friends and the community. I wasn't looking to move.

That always struck me as strange. I was happy and content and receiving job offers while others in the newsroom, who constantly complained and were miserable, never went anywhere.

That seems as true today as it was then. For some reason, whiners remain like barnacles on a ship. They're tough to remove because nobody else wants them.

BOOM! BOOM!

Remember, YOU control your attitude. If you have a fundamental difference with the way the company is operating, don't whine. Do something about it.

Tip No. 7:

Don't Put All Your Eggs In Your Career

There's an expression that goes: "Don't put all your eggs in one basket." It's the same with your career.

People often are so fixated with advancing in their organization that their careers are all they have in life. They don't take time to develop a personal life or outside interests.

That may be fine when everything is going well with your career, but what happens when it doesn't? What do you have left?

A woman who was a few years older than me was a talented manager within Gannett. She moved wherever the company asked and took on every duty the company asked.
She never developed a personal life. Her life was her work. She worked holidays, sometimes even scheduling meetings on those days, frustrating her managers who wanted to have a life.

Then about 20 years after starting her career, she met a man. Her life changed. She began to develop outside interests.

She became a more, well-rounded person.

When her career stagnated, she fortunately had something – and someone – to fall back on. She's now retired and happy with her life.

Imagine if she had never taken the time to develop a life outside of work. Don't let that happen to you.

Having outside interests often make you happier in your entire life. That can translate over to your work life. You're more grounded and more assured.

There's a friend of mine who has been extremely successful in his career. He has received promotions along the way and is a valuable member of his company. Still, he hasn't forgotten about the rest of his life. He is involved with his family and makes a point whenever possible to break away to attend his children's sporting events. He is involved in his church and in other activities.

"Having a life outside of work is essential," he said. "Being able to put down the phone and spend time with my family is crucial. Then when I do return to work issues I'm much more refreshed and revitalized."

Bosses often are more willing to accommodate you and your schedule if you're flexible and adjust your schedule when companies' needs require that. For example, your company might have certain times of the year when it is extremely busy such as accounting firms encounter during tax season. You likely will be expected to work additional days and hours. If you do it without complaint, your bosses will likely look more kindly when you need or want time off.

Bosses and companies will often go out of their way to accommodate valued employees. The goal is to make sure you are valued.

Your career is a big deal but so is your life. Make sure the company doesn't own all of it.

As Dr. Phil Tyler, a marketing professor at Rochester Institute of Technology told me while I was getting my MBA, he never heard any one on his or her death bed say, "I should have spent more time at the office."

BOOM! BOOM!

Having a good work/life balance is key. Make sure one of them doesn't get out of whack.

Tip No. 8:

Failure Isn't a Four-Letter Word

Al Neuharth is the retired CEO of Gannett and is best known as founder of *USA Today*. He died in 2013.

Neuharth had the vision that a national general-interest newspaper could thrive in the United States as it does elsewhere in the world. He staked his and the company's reputation on its success. On Sept. 15, 1982, *USA Today* launched and its impact changed the approach and look of newspapers throughout America.

Before he passed away, Neuharth wrote a column every Friday in *USA Today* offering his views on a variety of topics.

One of his columns, published on July 30, 1993, has stayed with me. The theme was lessons you can learn from failure.

In writing about the ruled suicide of Vince Foster, a close aide to then President Bill Clinton, Neuharth surmised that Foster, who died at age 48, couldn't handle his failures. After being a successful athlete, law school student and partner in a top law firm, Foster wasn't equipped when he got to Washington, and "a series of major-league errors overwhelmed this errorless minor-league player," Neuharth wrote.

"By contrast, criticism bounces off Clinton. He learned failure isn't fatal when he lost his re-election bid as governor of Arkansas at age 34."

Now, whether Neuharth's assessment of Foster's death is correct is not the point. The point is that failure is OK if you learn from it and can grow from it.

Neuharth wrote from experience. After serving in the U.S. Army during World War II and then attending the University of South Dakota, he and fellow alumnus Bill Porter founded *SoDak Sports*, a weekly newspaper devoted to covering the sports scene in South Dakota. Though initially popular, the publication went bankrupt in a year.

That didn't stop Neuharth. He went on to the *Miami Herald* and the *Detroit Free Press*, before joining Gannett and eventually becoming CEO.

Neuharth's taste of failure early on probably helped him during those days when many thought *USA Today* was just a pipe dream.

Sometimes when people are starting out or just into their careers, they feel as though they will always be a winner, that they will never experience failure. Many aren't prepared for what lies ahead. That's why it is important to have faith in yourself and to get off the deck when you're knocked down and to get back in the game.

Here's more from Neuharth's column:

"One such big failure teaches much more than a string of successes. If you're old enough to learn from it and young enough to try again. Under 40.

"Boomers or Busters, beware: As you approach 40 and haven't failed yet, hurry. Take some calculated big risks. And don't worry if they don't all work.

"The sky won't fall in. The moon and the stars will still be there. And the next time you reach for them, you're more likely to get them in your grasp."

The only way you are going to "get them in your grasp" is if you keeping trying. Many of the most successful people in the world have experienced failure along the way. All of you need to do is a Google search of "People Who Bounced Back from Failures" and you will be amazed at the people we consider geniuses such as Albert Einstein and Bill Gates who suffered serious setbacks. What they all had or have in common is the ability to keep believing in themselves and in their abilities.

Best-sellng author and renowned speaker Rita Davenport has given many presentations helping people deal with and overcome failure. She loves to dig into history and tell about this person:

- He finished eighth out of 13 candidates for the Illinois General Assembly in 1832.
- He tried again and was elected to the state legislature in 1834.
- His first romantic interest, Ann Rutledge, died in 1835.
- He broke off his engagement to Mary Todd and suffered another episode of depression in 1841. (He ended up marrying Mary Todd a year later).
- He was defeated in his run for Congress in 1843.
- He was elected to Congress in 1846.
- He chose not to run for re-election, applied for and was rejected as Commissioner of the General Land Office in 1849.
- He ran for and was defeated for U.S. Senate in 1854.

- He was defeated for nomination as Republican vice president in 1856.
- He lost a Senate campaign to Stephen Douglas in 1858.
- He was elected president in 1860.

He was Abraham Lincoln, considered one of the greatest presidents ever and whose Gettysburg Address during the Civil War became one of the most quoted speeches ever.

Lincoln never let failure stop him, it just slowed him down. As Lincoln said, "Always bear in mind that your own resolution to succeed is more important than any other."

BOOM! BOOM!

Failure isn't always bad; not learning from it is.

Tip No. 9:

What YOU Can Learn From My Failure

At age 37, after 15 wonderful years in Rochester, I accepted a promotion to become managing editor at the *Pensacola News Journal* in Florida. My company, Gannett, had been eager to promote me for years, but I liked working at the *Times-Union*. Other newspaper companies recruited me but I turned them down, too. My wife also had an excellent position as a sales representative for a health care company and was extremely successful. It didn't make sense to move.

In early 1993, my wife decided that she wanted to leave her job. That March, Rochester got hit with one of its infamous blizzards. More than 30 inches of snow came down in about a day. My headline in the T-U called it "March Madness" – a play on the ongoing NCAA basketball tournament. While bundled up plowing my driveway, I thought, "This weather is nuts. We've got to move to a warmer climate."

I detested the cold but had managed to tolerate it. This storm was the last straw, or more fittingly, the last snow flake.

The next day, I spoke with a friend at Gannett corporate. I mentioned about the snowstorm and how it might be time to move to a warmer climate.

The next day, a Gannett recruiter called and asked me about becoming managing editor in Pensacola. I didn't know much about the *News Journal* except for receiving clippings from that newspaper among others while writing a syndicated sports column for Gannett News Service and occasionally *USA Today*. I agreed to talk with the folks in Pensacola.

A few days later, I flew to Washington, D.C. to meet individually with the publisher and the editor. While talking with the publisher, her frustration with the editor became apparent. She didn't think the newsroom was that good or covered the important stories. With a background in finance, she thought her views about news got dismissed because she didn't have the credibility of someone who came up on the news side.

I should have seen all the "red flags." Pensacola also didn't have a great reputation within Gannett and had a string of editors and managing editors who had struggled there.

That didn't dissuade me. In my naiveté, I thought I could change that, thinking that because I had always been successful, I'll be successful there.

That was my first mistake.

A few weeks later, my wife and I flew to Pensacola. I met the staff and took a tour of the area. The white, sandy beaches and the pristine, calm Gulf of Mexico were quite an allure – especially for my wife – so I accepted the offer to become managing editor.

As we soon learned, the Gulf of Mexico wasn't always so pristine and calm – can you say hurricanes – and there were plenty of storm fronts surrounding my job.

The publisher became even more frustrated with the editor and that opinion reflected on the entire newsroom. I also didn't help the situation. I came in with a lot of grand ideas from Rochester and wanted to do big stuff. We launched a year-long series on the future of Pensacola but the newsroom wasn't talented enough to pull it off. I had overestimated the talent level of the staff which was a big mistake. I should have had them focus on improving basic reporting and editing. In baseball parlance, I should have gone for a bunch of singles instead of a home run.

That was my second mistake.

The rift between the publisher and the editor continued to grow. Less than two years later, he was gone just as Pensacola experienced a "double hit:" two hurricanes within two months. The first, Erin, caused massive destruction in Pensacola and surrounding areas. The second, Opal, devastated the beach.

One of the scariest times in my life came as we waited for Opal to hit. My wife and I lived in a condo on Pensacola Beach. That night, shortly after going to bed around 10, I got a call from the office that the storm was intensifying. We jumped out of bed, packed up a few things, drove into Pensacola and checked into a hotel near the office. I raced off to work and stayed until about 2:30 a.m. At the time, forecasters predicted Opal would land as a Category 1 storm with its eye headed toward New Orleans. I went back to the hotel to sleep.

At 5:30 a.m., I returned to the office only to learn that Opal had been upgraded to a Category 3 storm and was taking dead aim on Pensacola. Since the newspaper was in a flood plain, we needed to move newsroom operations. We had an arrangement with the local power company to use space in its secured building. We quickly gathered our staff to come and take shelter before the storm hit. This ended up like a scene from Noah's Ark as people brought not only themselves but their animals, too.

Time dragged as we waited for Opal to hit. Forecasters now predicted it would be a Category 5 (the worst). People trying to flee Pensacola got stuck in massive traffic jams.

Without an editor, I was in charge. Though my insides were churning and scared stiff, I tried to remain calm and reassure my staff. In all honesty, I feared for our lives.

Opal wound up hitting around noon as a Category 3, doing enormous damage. Once the storm passed and it was safe to go outside, we returned to the office and produced a newspaper for the next day.

There was one bright spot for me from Opal. They say the two happiest days in a boat owner's life are the day he buys the boat and the day he gets rid of it. When we moved to Pensacola, I thought it would be great to own a boat for water skiing. I soon learned that the Santa Rosa Sound was often too rough for skiing. It also was a big pain to put the boat in the water and then take it out, besides having to clean it afterward.

When my wife and I finally were allowed back on the beach days later to see how our condo fared, the boat had smashed into the storage shed and was ruined. Thankfully, it was covered by insurance.

My boat ownership days had mercifully come to an end.

Hurricane Opal wasn't the only drastic change in my life. I had a new editor.

The editor came from the idealistic world of corporate. She soon ran into the realistic world of a mid-size community daily. At corporate, sometimes they would roll out well-meaning initiatives without understanding the ramifications or the stress it put on newsrooms, especially smaller newsrooms.

For a while, the publisher and editor got along great. I admired the systematic way she approached issues and how she prioritized tasks. We would focus on an area, such as improving front-page headlines, until we saw real progress.

We did some great journalism during that period. I had spent a lot of time recruiting and hiring some talented young reporters and they, along with a couple of our veterans, produced some great stories. The newsroom won a number of national and state awards for investigative journalism. In 1997, corporate selected us as runner-up for Most Improved Newspaper, a huge turnaround.

The editor and the publisher eventually had a parting of the ways and she left.

In contrast, the editor's successor got along great with the publisher. He had worked in Pensacola before the publisher arrived and grew up on the Gulf Coast. He treated the publisher with respect, went out of his way to solicit her ideas and made her feel valued.

That changed the whole atmosphere. She started to appreciate the newsroom more and the value of the people in it. I got selected for one of the company's Newsroom Supervisor of the Year awards.

I also began working more closely with the publisher. The newspaper was inefficient in how it was utilizing newsprint – a huge cost for a newspaper – and she put me in charge of the project. We overhauled our procedures and began to make significant savings which pleased the publisher. She then also put me in charge of our community bi-weekly which gave me experience as a publisher in handling all facets of the operation.

We continued to excel in the newsroom as well and I got promoted to *The Arizona Republic* because of it.

BOOM! BOOM!

Your boss' relationship with his or her boss can be a huge factor in your success. If you have a supportive boss who has credibility with his or her boss, that can open opportunities for you.

YOUR BOOM! BOOM! TAKEAWAYS

_____

_____

_____

_____

_____

_____

_____

_____

_____

_____

_____

_____

_____

_____

CHAPTER 3
THE ROAD TO SUCCESS

Tip No. 10:
It's Not All About You

As someone who has hired many people, I'm always interested to see what candidates focus on during job interviews.

For example, when asking candidates why they want to work for a company, do they:

- o Focus on how the job will benefit them?
- o Focus on how hiring them will benefit the company?

That might seem like an easy question to answer but then you would be surprised how often people focus on themselves and not on the company.

Hiring people want the position to benefit the potential employee but they are more interested in making sure that person can do the job required and benefit the company.

In every job interview, make sure you frame your answers accordingly.

You need to convey how your skills and experience will translate to the position you are seeking.

At the end of the day, the hiring manager will look to answer one question: how will hiring you make his or her life better and the organization better? If the answer is yes, you are likely going to get offered the position.

This reality is burned into my memory. When visiting Gannett to discuss the managing editor position in Pensacola, FL, I met with many on the corporate staff. At the end of the day, in walking out of the building with a recruiter, I mentioned that if I went to Pensacola how much I could likely learn from the executive editor.

The recruiter stopped, looked at me and said, "He's not looking to train you. He's looking for you to do a job."

That editor and that recruiter had it right: in hiring me, what was in it for them, not for me.

A valuable lesson learned. That's why this is always important to remember when interviewing for a job.

One great way to prepare for interviews is to ask someone to role play with you.

Have that person ask you questions you might receive in an interview. Then you and the other person can evaluate your responses to see if they hit the mark.

If they don't measure up, keep doing it until you get your responses right. This also will take away some of the pressure when you finally interview with the hiring manager.

It's often surprising how little research job applicants do before going on job interviews. Here are some suggestions to help in that process:

- o Find out as much as possible about the people who are going to interview you. Check out LinkedIn or Google or another source to learn about their background and where they went to college. If people know that you took the time to learn about them, they will have a better impression of you.
- o Study the company's Web site, learning as much as possible about the organization and the businesses in which it competes.
- o Reach out to people in the company you might know to gain some background knowledge and perhaps learn the "inside scoop."

Finally, make sure in each interview to have questions for the hiring manager. It was always a big turn off at the end of an interview to ask the job applicant if she or he had any questions and have the person respond, "No, you covered everything." You know you didn't cover everything. The job applicant just didn't exhibit much curiosity about the job and the company.

You need to have thoughtful questions to ask. Here are some examples:

- What do you think are the most important skills a person needs to succeed in this company?
- What would you expect me to accomplish in my first year?
- What are the biggest opportunities for the company to take advantage of in the next few years?
- What are the biggest challenges that the company faces?
- How do you see the business evolving in the next five years? (This gives the hiring manager the idea that you are looking to have a career with the company).
- Reflecting on people you've hired for this position in the past, what do you find separates the outstanding ones from the good ones?

After each interview, follow up either via personal note or email, thanking the hiring manager for his or her time and detailing specific things you took from that interview. By being specific, the hiring manager will know that you tailored your note especially for him or her and that it's not a generic note you send.

Always remember, until you have a job offer, the balance of power is with the company.

BOOM! BOOM!

Make sure you convey to the hiring manager how hiring you will benefit the organization.

Tip No. 11:

Remember: Bosses are Human, Too

One major complaint employees often have about their bosses is that they never receive enough feedback.

- o **They're disappointed** when their good work isn't acknowledged.
- o **They're frustrated** when they don't think they are receiving enough support to succeed in their work.
- o **They're angry** when they get passed over for a promotion.

But consider this: How much feedback are you giving your boss?

Employees often forget that their bosses are human, too, with the same feelings and same insecurities that employees have.

So what should you do?

Make sure you give positive feedback to your boss when he or she helps you. Your boss is eager to know whether what he or

---

she said or did made a difference. Your boss also will be more inclined to help you in the future.

This doesn't mean gratuitous feedback. Most people can see through that. But sincere thanks can go a long way to developing a richer and more meaningful relationship with your boss.

It's one of those truisms of life – most people respond to positive feedback whether they are the boss or the employee.

While managing editor in Pensacola, I remember reading the performance evaluation an editor completed on one of our newer reporters. In her self evaluation, the reporter mentioned how she appreciated the times I had spent with her discussing stories and providing writing tips.

I was blown away. I had no idea that she felt that way. It made me feel good that she valued my ideas and encouragement. Who do you think I made a point to spend time with going forward?

There was a talented young sports writer in Pensacola whom I spent a lot of time helping. He soaked up the advice given and was always appreciative. It was rewarding to watch him develop as a reporter and a writer.

As a manager, you often work vicariously through your employees. In newspapers, for example, you're not writing the stories and often not making the sales. The satisfaction for a manager comes when you see your people succeed and know that you had a hand in their front-page story or their big sale.

One of the secrets of success in your career is learning your bosses' preferred communication style.

Here are some things to consider about your bosses:

- Do they prefer email, a phone call or an in-person visit?
- Do they have a best time of day to interact with them?
- Do they prefer a "just-the-facts" presentation or do they enjoy having a more-expansive conversation?
- Do they have a sense of humor? Do they want you to have a sense of humor?
- Do they care about your personal life?

These are the type of insights that are helpful to know about your boss. Once you adapt to that person's style, it's easier to have a better working relationship. Also, realize that you might interact with several different bosses all with different styles. You will need to adapt to those styles.

In Pensacola, one of my direct reports darted into my office first thing each morning to talk about non business stuff. He had done this with the former boss. This bothered me. I preferred spending my first half hour handling emails and preparing for the day. His visits disrupted my routine. Finally I told him that we would catch up later in the morning.

In Phoenix, my boss arrived early and the best time to catch him was before 8 a.m. when he headed into meetings. He was extremely busy, so when I needed to speak with him, it had to be extremely important and I needed to stay on message. If he wanted to have a longer discussion or bring up other topics, that was fine, but I was not going to initiate that.

The proliferation of emails has been a game changer. People now have access to you 24 hours a day. Be careful how you use it. Like a cigarette box, email accounts should come with a warning label:

Improper usage can be hazardous to your career.

Your boss – and others – might send plenty of emails, some that might aggravate you. Remember: never respond in anger or haste. Take time to collect your thoughts. If in doubt, write the email, save it and come back to it when you are less emotional.

Then you can decide if you still want to send it. Some of the best emails are ones you never send.

Emails are a great way to keep your boss informed and also provide a record of your correspondence. When you just have conversations with people, they can later deny saying something. If you have it in an email, you have documentation.

A good rule is if you have an important conversation with your boss or a colleague, follow up with an email outlining what was discussed. This is especially important if you have agreed to undertake a project and want to be clear on the parameters and the deadline.

Another reminder: in this era of texting, people often take short cuts in their communication. Don't do that in an email. These are business correspondence, not notes to a friend about where you are going to party this weekend. Make sure you use proper grammar and spell check the email. Too often, people laugh at bosses who use improper grammar or have mistakes in an email.

Don't forget: you're in a business setting. Don't mix your work life with your personal life. If you have personal emails to send, have a personal email account and don't use the company account.

Finally, my pet peeve regarding writing and responding to emails: Consider who needs to see the email or the response to an email. Some people have the frustrating habit of ccing: a bunch of people who don't need to get the email or the response. They instinctively hit reply all when reply all isn't necessary. All that does is clutter up people's emails.

There are plenty of stories out there on the internet about people who hit reply all who ended up regretting doing it. The reply and the reply all keys are close by in many email programs so it is always wise to check twice to make sure you are sending to the person or persons you want to have receive your email. Also be careful when forwarding an email that you don't hit reply. There also are plenty of disasters out there about people who made that mistake and ended up losing their job.

BOOM! BOOM!

If it's appropriate, make sure you tell your boss how much you appreciate him or her. He or she is more likely to become your advocate.

Tip No. 12:

Give Your Colleagues Positive Feedback

A successful business career is all about developing relationships. People often concentrate on developing relationships upward. Make sure also to develop those relationships among people at your level or those below your level.

They are often the people who can help you when you really need it.

In my position as vice president of community newspapers at *The Arizona Republic*, it was essential that I had strong working relationships with my peers. My success was often dependent on the quality of work of their staffs.

If your peers like and respect you, they will often go out of the way to help you. For example: when a breaking news story required pushing back the production deadline, my relations with the production department helped to get a later deadline.

This also worked in reverse. When production was in a jam, I would help them out by adjusting the deadlines so the newsroom finished its work earlier.

When you see peers doing great work, let them know. They are often surprised and appreciative when you pick up the phone to call them, send them an email or tell them in person. Many people think the only feedback they get is negative.

That's why after receiving great customer service on the phone, I'll often ask to speak to his or her boss so that the supervisor knows. As someone who occasionally dealt with irate phone callers, I appreciated hearing someone call to compliment one of my employees.

Being friendly and courteous to people isn't just the humane thing to do, it's also the wise thing to do. People are more inclined to help people they like. Try it and you might be amazed at the results.

Remember the adage: Treat others like you would want to be treated.

Another key to success is being able to work with others and not always dominating everything.

My inclination is to coordinate everything. In group settings, it's my nature to step up and organize things. That's fine, but it's also important to let others contribute and share the load.

This is a valuable lesson I learned while receiving my MBA: don't try to do everything.

In some classes, we had four-person study groups who would meet every Saturday and Sunday to work on projects. After working all week and going to classes at night, this was the last place I wanted to be. Going to the dentist for a root canal seemed less painful than this.

As part of our study group, we sat around a classmate's kitchen table and discussed what we needed to accomplish to complete a project.

In the past, I would have wanted to coordinate everything – make all the assignments and likely end up doing most of the work. But that just wasn't possible with my newspaper workload and taking two classes.

So when we divvied up responsibilities, I learned to keep my mouth shut on occasion and allow others to step up.

Sometimes the silence in the room was maddening. Sometimes I had to bite my lip from speaking. I would play a game with myself: how long could I go without opening my mouth. Eventually, others spoke up and agreed to do some of the tasks.

I had to learn that I didn't have to do everything and to trust that my teammates would complete their tasks and do them well.

This is so applicable in business situations. You're likely going to end up in groups working with your colleagues. Don't assume you have all the answers. Don't assume it's all up to you. Your colleagues likely have talents and skills that complement yours. They likely will have ideas that you wouldn't even have considered. Keep an open mind and you might be surprised at where the conversation will lead.

BOOM! BOOM!

Too often, Type A personalities can overwhelm a group. They don't allow others to participate or share ideas. Remember to encourage others to talk and contribute.

Tip No. 13:

Know Your Customer

My wife, Margaret, was an extremely successful medical sales representative. She developed great rapport with her customers and provided them awesome service before, during and after a sale.

Her secret to her success seems so simple but yet so difficult for many: She listened to what the customer wanted and figured out how to get that for them.

Too often in sales or in life, we are so busy talking that we fail to listen to the other person. We're so busy pitching our agenda that we never take time to hear their thoughts.

In going on sales presentations, sales reps were sometimes so fired up, so eager to talk about themselves and what the company could do for the customer, that they failed to determine the potential customer's needs. They didn't realize what they were pitching might be products or services the customer had no interest in buying.

Afterward, I had to remind the sales rep how important it was to engage the customer in conversation and to determine the customer's needs.

That's how my wife did it. She would go in and talk with potential customers about what they were looking for and what they thought of different products. Often the customer knew exactly what he or she wanted. Then it was up to my wife to figure out if she and her company could make that happen.

She also would try to get the customer to explain what problems or frustrations they had in doing their business in case her company had a product that might help ease the customer's burden.

Even if you never go into sales, this technique can be applied to so many other situations. Understanding others' needs – including your bosses – can go a long way in coming up with ways that you can help them fulfill those needs.

For example, you're asked to determine why there are cost overruns on a project. The first inclination might be to come in and start recommending ways the company can reduce costs. The better approach would be to come in and start talking with the people in the department. Once you build trust, often people on the front lines will tell you what the real problems are and might have ideas on how to reduce cost overruns. They feel empowered because you sought their opinion and will likely be more willing to make adjustments because they feel they have a stake in the solution.

Too often, people think of customers as just external customers – the people, for example, who are buying a product. Don't forget about the internal customers – the people you work with every day. It's important to know what makes them tick and what you need to do to get them as allies.

Don't also forget about non-verbal communication -- both yours and the person or people you are interacting with. Some research shows that the message you convey in a sales conversation is 55% body language and nonverbal communication, 38% tone of voice, and only 7% in the words that you use. Having a pleasant personality, smiling and showing interest in others goes a long way. Also learn to read other people's non-verbal cues. They often will indicate how interested they are in what you are communicating.

There's a great rule in life that can be applied to dealing with customers and with many other situations. That is the definition of insanity – doing the same thing over and over again and expecting different results.

It is as true today as when Albert Einstein supposedly said it. This is a great thing to remember when dealing with customers or many other situations.

One of my favorite stories from my wife came when she and her co-worker were leaving a hospital one day. They had met separately with different clients. He kept pushing a product that the customer refused to buy. My wife left with an order. When learning this, the co-worker shook his head and said he didn't get it. My wife simply said, "I just listened to what the customer wanted."

BOOM! BOOM!

Remember what the late Stephen Covey wrote as Habit 5 of his *7 Habits of Highly Successful People*: Seek first to understand, then to be understood.

Tip No. 14:

Know How to Close

There's a great movie to rent: *Glengarry Glen Ross*. The story revolves around four Chicago salesmen trying to sell undesirable real estate at inflated prices. To push the salesmen, the supervisor announces a sales contest. The winner gets a Cadillac. Second place gets a set of steak knives. Third and fourth place: get pink slips and we aren't talking lingerie.

Talk about a harsh contest. But talk about reality. In your business career, if you can't close, you likely won't keep your job long.

Closing isn't just for sales people. It can apply to anyone in business.

For example:

o   **Can you close people on your ideas?** You might have a great way to save the company money, but if you can't get others to buy into it, your idea will go nowhere.

- Can you get people to help you? You might need assistance in gathering information for a project, but if you can't get people to help, the project could end up a failure.
- Can you get people to talk with you? You might be covering a story and you need to talk to the victim of a crime, but if you can't get the person to talk, you might not get the story.

Remember, while you might not be able to get people to buy into your ideas, get people to help or to get people to talk with you, there are people out there who can. These are the people who are going to get promoted and succeed.

A friend of mine, Joe Scotto, started out as a newspaper copy editor but a few years later went into sales. He became skilled at selling Yellow Pages advertising and was one of his company's top performers. Joe knew what it took to succeed.

"Regarding your question on what skill or work ethic makes a salesperson successful, that is an easy one for me, that is the ability to close," he said. "Many managers believe that hard work is the key, however, that is a great attribute to possess, but the closer is the true superstar. The sales rep that helps the customer make a decision on a consistent basis is the winner. Many reps give great presentations, but can't close. Show me a closer, and I'm sure they are a high earner. They are able to see more customers, make more sales, and are productive individuals."

Joe knows how to close. A former colleague of my wife's didn't. He was working on a lucrative deal and had finally convinced a doctor to spend the afternoon with him out on his boat. It was a beautiful afternoon with the sun glimmering on the water. He was telling my wife later about what a good time they had when she asked him, "what about getting him to buy the product?" All he could say sheepishly was, "The product never came up." He had blown a perfect opportunity to land some lucrative business.

In *Glengarry Glen Ross*, there's a great scene when the boss is talking to his beleaguered sales staff:

"These are the new leads. These are the Glengarry leads. And to you they're gold, and you don't get them. Why? Because to give them to you would be throwing them away. They're for closers."

Are you a closer? Would the boss give you the leads?

In going after the close, don't sell yourself short. Sometimes people might be able to spend or do more than you might first expect.

A friend of mine was president and CEO of a health care system in the Southeast. He was out fundraising for a new hospital. He set up an appointment with a wealthy woman. They had a pleasant conversation for about 45 minutes before he asked the big question:

"Would you be willing to donate $1 million for the new hospital?"

The woman looked at him and said, "Sure."

The two continued talking and all the while the CEO had this gnawing thought that he had left money on the table, that he hadn't asked the woman for enough money.

Finally, he couldn't hold it in any longer, so he looked at her and asked:

"If I had asked you to donate $2 million, would you have done it?"

The woman looked at him, smiled and said: "But you asked for $1 million."

The CEO had learned his lesson.

In baseball parlance, don't settle for a single, when you might get a double, triple or home run. When you're in the batter's box, think big.

Another good rule to remember is not to stereotype people. Just because they might not look like they have money, doesn't mean they don't have money.

A manager of a high-end department store in Scottsdale told this story. In previous markets, he, his managers and his sales staff could pretty much tell by the way people dressed how wealthy they were and if they could afford to buy clothes in that store. If the people fit that description, the sales people went out of their way to make the people feel at home, provide them drinks and cater to their every whim. If they didn't fit that description, the sales staff didn't "waste their time" on them and hoped they soon would leave the store.

In Scottsdale, the manager said, it was tougher to stereotype people because some people dress more casually. One night a woman entered the store not that nicely dressed. She demanded VIP treatment and the staff thought they were getting played. They were annoyed. "There's no way this woman is going to buy anything," they thought. "She's just wasting our time."

How wrong those sales people ended up being. In a couple of hours, the "not that nicely dressed woman" walked out after spending more than $10,000.

The manager said they had learned their lesson and were going to need to change their approach: "From now on, we're going to have to treat every one nice."

BOOM! BOOM!

Being able to close isn't just important in sales. It's important in life if you want to get what you desire.

Tip No. 15:

Be Willing to Change

One of my newspaper publishers in Rochester was David Mack. In meetings, he occasionally told the story about what happened to the Penn Central railroad.

"The reason they went out of business," he said, "was because they thought of themselves as a railroad company and not a transportation company."

Mack told the story to remind everyone why it was important for companies to evolve. He used to tell his employees that we were no longer a newspaper company, but a communications company and that we could provide people with information besides the printed form.

As we soon learned, the newspaper business changed dramatically, especially with the growth of the Internet. Now there is a generation of people who prefer to receive news on their smart phones instead of in newspapers.

That's why it is extremely important in your career to continue to learn new things and expand your talents. The skills you might need in five years are skills you might not possess today.

People who want to evolve and succeed are those who will figure out how to get the needed skills. They are people who won't just depend on their company to provide that training. They are proactive, seeking training opportunities and keeping up through reading and conversations about the latest technology.

Companies are looking for people who embrace change, who are willing to try new things, who are willing to take risks. They are the people who will be in demand. Silicon Valley is full of millionaires who did so.

One of those who embraced change is Mike Mika. We worked together at the *Pensacola News Journal*. He had spent his career in the newsroom and had been a city editor before becoming business editor. He could have stayed in the newsroom and had a successful career.

But Mike realized that the newspaper business was changing even back in the mid-1990s. Up until then, the only way for a newspaper to distribute information was in a printed form. As an early adapter to technology, he realized the importance that the internet and computers would play on culture – and the newspaper industry.

He welcomed the opportunity to work with the publisher on an audio text project. Audio text offered recorded news and information on the phone to consumers who dialed a three-digit number. He worked for 11 months on a business plan and then ultimately concluded that the company had missed its chance to be a player in that platform.

Mike realized there was one area that the company hadn't missed its chance – the ability to figure out the newspaper's role on the web.

Soon after, Mike's career came to a crossroads. There's an expression "put your money where your mouth is." Mike had to "put his career where his mouth was." Would he be willing to give up a successful career in the newsroom to take a flier on developing a business model and create one of the first websites for Gannett?

We spent time talking about his decision. The more we talked, the more he realized that this was the opportunity to be on the cutting edge of something that could radically change how news is delivered.

Mike took the leap and never looked back. He helped the newspaper and Gannett build and grow its digital strategy and had a successful second career in this field.

In your career, you might face a similar crossroad. Being willing to assess and then take a risk might be the difference between a stagnating or flourishing career.

Technological change will continue at a rapid pace. Companies to remain successful are always going to need to adjust their business plans and take advantage of opportunities. If they don't, they will end up like the Penn Central railroad. They are going to need people willing to step up and embrace opportunities.

There's a great quote from former British Prime Minister Harold Wilson, speaking to the Consultative Assembly of the Council of Europe in Strasbourg, France in 1967:

"He who rejects change is the architect of decay. The only human institution which rejects progress is the cemetery."

BOOM! BOOM!

Are you willing to embrace change or are you headed to the cemetery?

Tip No. 16:

Don't Get Too High, Too Low

As a boy, I remember reading an article in *The Sporting News* about a baseball player's philosophy toward hitting. He said he didn't get too high when he went 4-for-4 or too low when he went 0-for-4.

That's good advice for life. Often, it's easy to get pumped up when everything seems to go your way. Then, it's easy to get depressed when nothing seems to go your way.

The key is to have a strong inner core and not let outside events impact who you are or your belief in yourself.

Too often in life, you will experience the teeter-totter effect. For a while you will be up, and then you will be down. How you handle that will determine the type of person you are and how you cope with adversity.

You will see this often in business. A person, whom bosses think is fantastic one year, is on the outs the next year.

There's an advertising director that I know. Her team exceeded goal one year. She received a promotion and everyone loved her. The next year, her team failed to achieve goal and the sniping began.

Did that person in one year go from being brilliant to being stupid? No. Sometimes economic and personnel changes can affect performance.

As former President John F. Kennedy said, "Victory has a thousand fathers, but defeat is an orphan."

Remember: exceeding goal covers up a myriad of sins; missing goal exposes everything.

That's why it's important not to get too high or too low. People who tell you how great you are when you are on top are often the same people who tell you how lousy you are when you are on the bottom.

It's important to stay true to yourself.

One way to succeed in business is to realize when you are most productive. Some people are better in the morning, some are night owls. Knowing who you are is important.

If you know you are most productive in the morning, make sure you schedule your most important tasks then. If you work better in the evening, make sure you are doing those tasks then.

Authors of business books often write about ranking priorities as either A, B or C with A priorities the most important. It's essential to spend your most productive time on the A priorities. You can work on the B and C priorities in your off-peak time.

I'm a morning person. It comes from working 15 years at jobs that required being at work by 5:30 a.m. That was a radical departure from college when I stayed up half the night and refused to take a class before 9 a.m.

Now if there is something important to do, I get up early. The mornings are calm, my mind is alert and I can focus.

That doesn't work for everyone. There are friends of mine who love working late in the evenings because that's their peak time.

The key is to know yourself.

BOOM! BOOM!

Make sure you know when you are most productive and, when possible, schedule your most important work around that.

Tip No. 17:

Hang in There

They are called phases in your life. These are when your environment drastically changes and your comfort level is disrupted.

One of the toughest periods in people's lives is often the first semester in college. They are going from high school where, by the end of senior year, they know a lot of people and are extremely comfortable with the environment.

Now, especially if they go out of town and leave friends, college can seem daunting. They're filled with anxiety:

- "Who are these people? They're all strangers.
- "Will I like my roommate? Will I like living in a dorm?
- "What about the food? No longer will my mom be around to make my favorite meal.
- "Can I keep up with the work in college? I did well in high school but this is college."

So many questions, so many concerns. It's no wonder some freshmen get depressed and drop out.

My nephew is a perfect example of this. He was so bummed after graduating from high school. He loved high school and couldn't believe it could get better than that. He and his friends were going to different colleges and he realized things would never be the same.

I tried to console him and to tell him to just wait.

"Believe it or not, in a couple years, you'll be eager to be going back to college," I told him. "All of your friends will be there and that will be the center of your universe. When you come home, you'll see your high school friends and realize you don't have that much in common with them any more. You're all off to different schools and different situations. Once you've relived high school life for the 100th time, you'll realize you've all moved on."

He didn't believe me, but sure enough he went off to college and eventually started to love it. Some friends he made there are friends for life.

My college roommate's daughter went off to college a few years ago. She didn't want to go and was depressed about leaving home.

My how things changed. When she returned home after her sophomore year, she started counting the days toward when she would head back to college.

The key lesson is to hang in there. Too often, some freshmen just can't deal with homesickness and need to leave.

If you can hang in there and make it through the first semester, you may realize that:

- o   Those "strangers" are now your friends.
- o   Your roommate is pretty decent, though he or she has a strange taste in music.
- o   The food is bearable but certainly nothing like your mom's.
- o   You can get good grades if you apply yourself.

Just like going to college is a major phase in someone's life, so is starting your first – or a new – job.

The same unsettledness you felt then, you feel again.

The key is to look upon it as a challenge and to focus on the positives of your new environment.

After a while, just like when going to college, you'll get into the swing.

BOOM! BOOM!

Hang in there. The first few weeks or months in a new job can seem overwhelming, especially if you're moving to a new town.

Tip No. 18:
Don't Beat Yourself Up

I'm amazed at how many people put themselves down. They criticize themselves for the smallest things, from forgetting to do some task, to not staying in touch with a friend.

Those people forget about all the good things they do and focus on what they didn't do. They always see the glass as half empty, not half full.

My advice: don't beat yourself up. There are plenty of people in your life willing to do that for you. They're quite eager to point out your faults and shortcomings.

Don't help them do it.

It's OK to internalize your frustrations and to learn and grow from them. But don't go around verbalizing all your shortcomings.

Sometimes putting yourself down can be a self-fulfilling prophesy. If you keep repeating negative thoughts, they'll often happen.

This can occur on the golf course when someone will predict that they will hit a bad shot and then do it. They'll slam their club down, swear and call themselves an idiot. What did they expect? They predetermined the outcome.

A friend of mine is a master of this. He verbally flogs himself often over what he sees are his mistakes.

He also puts himself down in meetings when giving a presentation. By minimizing his own views and his experiences, he marginalizes the impact he has on the group. If he doesn't think what he's saying is important, then why should others think what he's saying is important.

When presenting, know your subject matter and speak confidently. Often it's not the words that have the greatest impact, it's the way those words are spoken.

Also, keep in mind, how you react to situations is crucial.

In Rochester, there was a photo editor who consistently shot himself in the proverbial foot – and he wasn't shooting it with his camera. His words provided all the ammunition.

The sad part was, he never grasped how bad that made him look.

During the morning news meetings, the editor and the managing editor often would attend. The news meetings provided a forum for the editors to discuss that day's newspaper and plan stories and photos for the next day.

Occasionally, the editor would offer a story suggestion that would include needing a picture taken.

It didn't matter the photo idea, the photo editor's reaction was usually the same. He would lean in to the table and in a dismissive voice say, "We can't do that. The photo book is filled."

The room would go silent. The editor, clearly annoyed, would tell him to go check the photo book and get the picture assigned.

The photo editor, now clearly annoyed himself, would go back, complaining along the way about how it was nearly impossible to juggle all these assignments and how no one understood his job.

Soon, after calming down, the photo editor was able to adjust the photo schedule and get the picture the editor wanted assigned.

He thought he was a hero for doing it. He didn't realize he was anything but a hero.

He never seemed to grasp this even after I would repeatedly tell him:

"Don't you get it? You look bad either way. If you go back to the photo studio, adjust the schedule and get the photo assigned, the editor still thinks that you didn't want to take the photo and that you had to be forced into doing it. If for some legitimate reason you can't change the photo schedule, the editor thinks you didn't try hard enough and that you sabotaged his idea."

That's why it is so important how you react to ideas from your bosses or your colleagues. Your initial reaction to ideas is sometimes what people remember most.

BOOM! BOOM!

Don't put yourself down and don't give people reasons to put you down.

Tip No. 19:

When in Doubt, The Word to Use

Comedian Arte Johnson brought laughs most every Monday night during the late 1960s and early 1970s. He appeared on the hit TV series *Rowan & Martin's Laugh-In* and portrayed a German soldier who would say, "Very Interesting."

Interesting – a great word to use when you're not sure how you feel about a certain situation or issue. This is one of those words that can be taken as a positive or negative. Using it also can buy you time as you formulate your thoughts.

For example, a boss or a colleague presents you with an idea. They want to launch a new product that could require lots of your time. Your immediate reaction is negative, but you don't want to come off as negative.

Instead, you can say, "That's an interesting concept." Your boss or colleague will think that you're keeping an open mind to the idea while you hear more.

Eventually you may explain why you don't like the idea, but by saying "interesting," you bought yourself some more time.

One of my favorite stories about the word interesting came while program chair of my Rotary Club. The executive director said a club member had for years put on a St. Patrick's Day program. I thought, "That's one less program for me to schedule."

The day of the program came but I couldn't stay to see it. The next week, I was talking with a fellow club member.

He said, "That was an interesting program last week."

"Oh," I said, "you liked it?"

"No," he said, "I didn't say that. I said it was interesting."

Indeed he had. And thus I learned the power of the word interesting.

BOOM! BOOM!

Come up with an all-purpose word you can use when you want to buy yourself time before sharing an opinion.

Tip No. 20:

#MeToo and You

Let's get one thing clear: sexual or any type of harassment in the workplace is not acceptable under any circumstance.

Though isolated, sexual harassment for years was the dirty little secret in the workplace. People knew it was going on, but few spoke up about it. Many perpetrators thought it was "boys being boys" and many victims thought it was best to suffer in silence or risk possibly derailing their careers.

Thankfully, in this era of Harvey Weinstein, the Hollywood producer accused of sexual harassment and assault, things are changing. No longer are some sexual harassers getting away with it and some victims no longer refusing to speak up.

"For too long, survivors of sexual assault and harassment have been in the shadow," said Tarana Burke, founder of the #MeToo movement in a statement after *Time* magazine chose the #MeToo Movement's "Silence Breakers" as Person of the Year for 2017. "We had been afraid to speak up, to say '#MeToo' and seek accountability. For many, the consequences of doing so have been devastating."

So what should you do?

If you have been or become a victim of sexual or any other kind of harassment, don't just take it. Take action. There are plenty of articles on the web that provide solid advice and step-by-step instructions upon how to proceed. Harassment can come from bosses, co-workers, customers or non-employees so each case is different and how best to address the issue will change. The best suggestion is to document what occurred so you will have a record of the transgression.

This is where a mentor or a close confidant outside of the company can be vital in helping you make smart decisions on how best to proceed. The person also can provide moral and emotional support.

Workplace harassment is a form of discrimination that violates Title VII of the Civil Rights Act of 1964, the Age Discrimination in Employment Act of 1967 (ADEA) and the Americans with Disabilities Act (ADA) of 1990.

The Equal Employment Opportunity Commission (EEOC) defines harassment as unwelcome verbal or physical behavior that is based on race, color, religion, sex (including pregnancy), gender/gender identity, nationality, age (40 or older), physical or mental disability or genetic information.

Harassment becomes unlawful where:

- Enduring the offensive conduct becomes a condition of continued employment.
- The conduct is severe or pervasive enough to create a work environment that a reasonable person would consider intimidating, hostile or abusive.

The key to a safe workplace environment is to think before you speak, to think before you act.

- You might think that joke you want to tell is funny but will it offend someone?
- You might have this email you want to forward but is it in good taste?
- You might have some prank you want to pull on a co-worker but should you really do it?

The workplace is not a clubhouse. It's a professional environment and should be treated as such. No one should have to endure a hostile work situation.

One offshoot of the #MeToo movement is the recognition that companies function best when both men and women are involved in decision making. Too often organizations have been led by just white men.

There's an excellent book published in early 2018 by Joanne Lipman, former editor at *USA Today* called *That's What She Said: What Men Need to Know (and Women Need to Tell Them) About Working Together*. The book stresses how when men and women work together, the results are often better than when men just work alone. Diversity in gender, along with diversity in age, backgrounds, thinking and ideas enhance results.

The best rule to remember regarding harassment: if in doubt, don't.

BOOM! BOOM!

Knowing what to do and not do in the workplace is important. If you aren't sure, seek guidance.

Tip No. 21:
Trust Your Gut

These are three of the most important words to remember in your professional and your personal life – trust your gut. Not trusting your instincts can often be to your peril.

In golf, wanting to hit another shot after the first one goes errant is called a mulligan. Unfortunately in life you don't always get a mulligan.

I remember working as a summer intern on the news copy desk of the *Times-Union*. I had won a Newspaper Fund Scholarship and, after two weeks of training at Virginia Commonwealth University, headed to my 10-week internship in Rochester.

The copy desk consisted of a bunch of men, some old enough to be my grandfather. I didn't know whether to call them Mr., Sir or by their first name.

My boss was Mike Lewis. He was called the slot editor because he reviewed the copy editors' work before sending it to the composing room for typesetting.

Shortly into my internship, I was editing a story one morning. Part of it didn't make sense. I can't remember the story, just what happened next. I thought to myself, "These facts seem strange" but I finished editing the story and sent it on to Mike Lewis.

A few minutes later he started reading the story. He soon looked up and asked me about the part of the story that I had questioned.

I'll always remember what I told him and, more importantly, what HE told me.

I said to him: "Gee, I wondered about that too."

He stared at me, then said: "And what did you do about it?"

Unfortunately, I had done nothing.

My gut told me a part of the story didn't make sense and I didn't act. That bugged me for days but the lesson was learned.

When reflecting on my career, often the decisions I regret the most are those when I failed to trust my instincts, to trust my gut.

Here's one example that comes to mind when I did trust my gut and was thankful afterward. We were publishing a special "Good News" section, one that spotlighted the good news, good people and good things in the Northeast Valley of the greater Phoenix area. The cover story was about the magnificent McDowell Mountain preserve. Taxpayers had acquired the land by paying additional sales tax.

I told the editors to show me the section cover when it was ready. Late one afternoon, they came to get me. The cover photo was a spectacular view of the McDowell Mountains with the city in the distance. In the foreground, almost silhouetted, was this woman.

At first glance, my eyes focused on the woman. "Is she dressed?" I asked. From the image, it was hard to tell. The editor said she was and that the design editors loved the shot.

My gut instincts went into high alert. I thought, if we publish this cover, it's going to blow up in our faces. All people will remember from this "Good News" section is that there was a potentially nude woman on the cover.

I explained my reasoning and told the editor to find another photo. We ended up using one taken at dusk with the McDowell Mountains in the foreground and the lights of Scottsdale in the background. The picture helped set the right tone for the section.

The cover headline said: "Our Gem: The Preserve."

Imagine if we had published that headline on the initial cover. Readers would have thought we were saying that the woman was "Our Gem."

BOOM! BOOM!

Learn to trust your gut. It often will steer you right.

Tip No. 22:

It's the "Little Things" That Count

Dr. Phil Tyler taught Advanced Marketing Management, my marketing capstone MBA class. This was a grueling class and our final team project required lots of time and effort.

Fortunately, Dr. Tyler made the class more bearable. He deeply cared about his students and willingly shared his extensive business experience.

Throughout the years, we've stayed in touch, often discussing and sometimes commiserating about our favorite NFL team, the New York Giants.

Dr. Tyler is a delight to talk with because he's so positive and full of solid insights. He has always taken an interest in me and my career and always provided great advice.

In finalizing this book, I wanted to get his feedback. As always, he came through big time. He called them "little things" that can make a big difference in someone's career and life:

These "little things" are so important that I created an additional tip to include them:

- o **The importance of a smile** — if you see someone without a smile, give her/him one of yours. There are enough pouty people in the world. People are drawn to happy people and one way to show happiness is by smiling.
- o **The importance of a firm handshake.** There's plenty of research that shows having a firm handshake helps make a great first impression for both men and women. This doesn't mean putting another person's hand in a vise grip. It means shaking hands with feeling. A weak handshake is a big turnoff. There once was a sports reporter I knew whose handshake was like a dead fish. Don't let that be you.
- o **The importance of eye contact.** Maintaining eye contact shows you're interested in the person you're talking with which reflects well on you. Also, by looking someone in the eye, it gives that person the feeling that you're confident in what you're saying. People often will listen to you more intently and take you more seriously.
- o **The importance of using people's names.** Legendary self-improvement author and speaker Dale Carnegie said it best more than 50 years ago: "There's no sound on earth as sweet to a person as the sound of their own

name." A tip to help you is when you meet someone for the first time: repeat back his or her name and then try to associate that name with someone or something. One warning: if you can't remember a person's name, don't guess. That might seem obvious but I knew someone who routinely called people by their wrong name. Talk about a turn off.

o **And of special importance** — really LISTEN when you are talking with someone. This is a skill that is so important to master. If people think you are interested in what they are saying, they will have a higher opinion of you. Often times, by active listening, you can pick up insights about the person you didn't even know. Remember: you never learn anything when you're speaking.

BOOM! BOOM!

As you can read, these aren't "little things." These "little things" could have a big impact on your career success.

YOUR BOOM! BOOM! TAKEAWAYS

_____

_____

_____

_____

_____

_____

_____

_____

_____

_____

_____

_____

_____

_____

_____

CHAPTER 4
TAKING CARE OF YOURSELF

Tip No. 23:

YOU Control Your Happiness

In one of my first visits to Phoenix, I attended a sports editors' convention at the Arizona Biltmore. One of the first presenters was best-selling author and renowned speaker Rita Davenport.

She recounted the story about a 23-year-old newlywed who was so miserable. That newlywed was her.

"I cried the first six weeks after getting married," she said. "I thought my husband would come home and sprinkle happy dust on me."

She had gotten married and immediately moved from Tennessee to Florida where her husband was in the space program. She didn't have a friend, she didn't have a job, she didn't have a life. She felt lonely and sorry for herself.

One day she went out to get the mail. The postman was putting the mail in the different slots when he looked at her.

"Ma'am, you don't look happy?" he said.

"My husband doesn't make me happy," she said and then proceeded to tell her tale of woe.

The postman stopped her. He looked at her and said: "Ma'am, you're only going to be as happy as you make up your mind to be."

His words struck to the core.

"My whole life changed at that moment," she said.

As Rita Davenport learned, and as she has been teaching people throughout the world for years, only you can control your happiness.

Rita started to reach out to people and took responsibility for her life.

As she says, happiness is based on a choice. You can't control what others do or say, but you can control your response to them.

Since that experience, Rita has spent her life giving seminars, encouraging people to take control of their life – and their happiness.

She developed eight rules for happy living:

1. Get into the happiness habit.
2. Declare war on negative feelings.
3. Strengthen your self-image.
4. Learn how to laugh.
5. Dig out your buried treasures.
6. Help others. What are you capable of doing that would benefit someone else?
7. Seek activities that will make you happy. What do you enjoy ?
8. Learn forgiveness. Who do you need to forgive?

As she says, "Remember the secret of happiness is good health and a short memory!"

BOOM! BOOM!

In your career, you're the only one who can make you happy. Don't give others the power to control your happiness.

Tip No. 24:
You're Not Alone

In life, we sometimes think that we are the only ones experiencing a certain feeling or emotion. For example, we forget that others feel nervous before taking a test or presenting before a big group.

This reality struck home one night while getting my MBA from Rochester Institute of Technology. The finance professor got off on some topic that left me baffled.

As an undergraduate, I likely would not have said a word. I would have assumed that I was the only one who didn't understand the professor.

But here I was in graduate school, tired from working all day and going to school at night. After about 10 minutes, I couldn't stand it. I raised my hand, told the professor that I didn't have a clue of what he was talking about and asked him to explain. He went back and more clearly articulated the subject matter.

About 15 minutes later, we took our break. Outside class, seven students individually came up to thank me for asking the professor to explain himself. They didn't know what he was talking about either.

We often miss out on understanding issues or processes by not being willing to ask questions. We fear that we might sound stupid so we just sit back and not speak up.

In the future, be willing to ask for explanations if you don't understand something. Remember, you're probably not alone.

One trait to develop is how to handle all that you've got going on – to strive not to get overwhelmed.

Football coaches are notorious for saying, "We take them one game at a time."

To fans, that sometimes seems ridiculous: "Come on, you've got to be thinking about that big game with your undefeated rival in three weeks."

To coaches, it's almost a survival instinct. They just want to focus on what's directly ahead of them – the game that week – because it can often seem daunting to look too far into the future.

That philosophy of "taking them one game at a time" resonated with me while in graduate school. With work and school, I always felt overwhelmed.

RIT operated on the quarter system so classes went for 11 weeks. I used to live my life in 11-week increments. Here was my thought process:

- At the beginning of the fall term: "Just make it to Thanksgiving. The semester will be over and I'll get a one-week break."
- Then, "Just make it through the three weeks of classes to Christmas and then I'll have two weeks off for the holidays."
- Then, "Just make it for eight weeks. The semester will be over and I'll get a one-week break."
- Then, "Just make it for 11 weeks. The spring semester will be over and I'll get a one-week break."
- Then finally during the summer, "Just make it for 11 more weeks and then I'll have a couple weeks off before fall semester begins."

Even thinking of life in 11-week increments seemed overwhelming. There was so much that needed to get done with school – plus work – that it could be depressing.

So each week, I would just focus on what needed to get accomplished that week with both my job and with my classes. Looking at it in smaller chunks made it seem more bearable. It's like the line about eating the elephant. It's better to eat it one bite at a time.

This philosophy holds true in your work life. Sometimes if you dwell on all that needs to be accomplished, it's easy to get overwhelmed. If you focus on the task at hand, it can seem more bearable.

At a race track, they put blinders on horses when they don't want them distracted. Sometimes, we need to wear blinders so we can just focus on the task at hand.

BOOM! BOOM!

Jim Memmott, a former managing editor in Rochester, offered some good advice, "Focus on the battles, not on the war."

Tip No. 25:

Forget a Dog, Get a Mentor

There's an old saying, "If you want a friend, get a dog."

Here's a new saying, "If you want to succeed in your career, get a mentor."

A mentor can play a valuable role in your life. He or she can provide career guidance and also can be there during your highs and lows. A mentor can offer an objective opinion not swayed as much as you may be by individuals and situations. To paraphrase a popular expression, a mentor can help you see the forest when all you can see are a bunch of trees.

John Calipari, the highly successful men's basketball coach at the University of Kentucky, shares this story about the value of having someone who will tell it to you straight. Imagine there's a 100-piece marching band parading down a field. Halfway down, 99 members turn left while you turn right. Your family and friends would likely say, "What are those other 99 doing?" A good mentor or coach would say, "What are you doing going the wrong way?"

My former colleague in Pensacola, Sherry Hartnett, knows the value of mentors. Since joining the University of West Florida business school, the now Dr. Hartnett started an executive mentor program in 2012. The program matches students with business executives for one-on-one mentoring that provides particular attention to the students' professional development needs.

"Workforce readiness in college students occurs when graduates have core basic knowledge and the ability to apply their skills in the workplace," she said.

In doing her research on the topic, she found:

- Employers typically want new hires to have the requisite skills for their positions and the ability to quickly acclimate and be valuable in the work environment on day one.
- Business executives place a high value on the applied skills—sometimes referred to as soft skills— of professionalism, communication, leadership, critical thinking, and self-confidence.

- Soft skills—which are needed to communicate, problem-solve, collaborate, and organize—are becoming more important for success as the workplace evolves socially and technologically.
- Workforce readiness and job success depend on social, personal, and applied cognitive skills.

Hartnett thought that a mentoring program – pairing business executives and leaders with soon-to-be graduating students – could provide those students with a competitive edge and improve their chances for success in their work careers.

"In addition to the individualized mentoring provided by the business executives, the program also offers students an opportunity to put the applied skills they are learning from their mentors into practice," she said. "This is accomplished through activities such as networking and training events that students and mentors are encouraged to attend."

The mentoring program has proven extremely successful.

Hartnett realized from the start how much the students would benefit from the mentorship program. What she soon realized and continues to realize is how much the mentors enjoy the program and the satisfaction they receive from participating.

"Having a mentor can be invaluable for your career," said Michael Krueger, one of my mentees. "A mentor will be able to tell you if your professional ideas would actually work in the real world and will also be able to give you tips on how to make that jump from college grad to a young professional. The mark of any good mentor will be one able to tell you when your ideas are good. The mark of a great mentor will be one who challenges your ideas in the hopes of shaping them into even better action plans."

A mentor can help at any stage of your career. Top executives even hire management consultants to provide outside advice to help them succeed.

If you don't think you need a mentor, ask yourself these questions:

- Do you think you are already smart enough?
- Do you have all the answers to all the situations you encounter?
- Do you fear receiving objective feedback?

BOOM! BOOM!

Finding the right mentor could provide big career dividends for you now and going forward.

Tip No. 26:

Only One Person Knows the Truth – You!

In school, I rarely talked about my grades. To me, it was ridiculous to do so. The only person the grades meant something to was me. I was the only one who knew how much – or how little – effort I put in to receiving the grade.

I remember my sophomore year in college. I received an A in Roman Civilization and did almost nothing. I busted my butt and received a B in Spanish.

If someone was looking at my grades, they would likely say: "Great work in Roman Civ. Too bad you didn't do as well in Spanish." That person wouldn't have a clue about how much more satisfied I was with that B in Spanish than that A in Roman Civilization.

That's the way it is in life. Only you know how much effort you put into your job or into your personal life.

Take sales for example. Some periods you might get lucky and land a couple of accounts that you put little effort into acquiring. You exceed goal and your manager is happy. Then another period comes and you're out hustling, making presentations and developing relationships. You end up missing goal and your manager is upset. Deep down, you know you worked much harder in that period than in the period you made goal. You know that that hard work will pay off in subsequent periods.

The only person who knows the truth about how you're living your life is the person staring at you in the mirror each day. That's why it's important to hold yourself accountable.

Here are some questions you might ask yourself:

o Am I really extending myself, pushing myself to develop my skills and to get better?

o If I were going to grade my effort, what would I honestly give myself? Is that the grade I want?

o Do I really just want to coast through life or do I want to make a difference?

o What are three things I could implement that would make a huge difference in my life and how I impact others?

Doing a self-assessment such as this is hard. It's not for the faint of heart. It's much easier to look into the mirror and tell yourself that you're great.

But that wouldn't be the truth and WE KNOW the truth.

Albert Einstein probably said it best: "Man must cease attributing his problems to his environment, and learn again to exercise his will – his personal responsibility."

BOOM! BOOM!

In life you are accountable to yourself. You might fool other people, but you can't fool yourself. You know the effort – or lack of effort – you are putting forth.

Tip No. 27:

Take Time to Appreciate the Good Times

There's a pithy quote, author unknown:

"We are so often caught up in our destination that we forget to appreciate the journey, especially the goodness of the people we meet on the way. Appreciation is a wonderful feeling, don't overlook it."

How true. Often we don't appreciate what we have until it goes away.

That is also true in your career. If you are in a job that you love, with people you enjoy working with, appreciate it. Enjoy those times.

Unfortunately, they probably won't last. Even if you don't change, people and situations will change around you.

As managing editor in Pensacola, I helped build a talented staff over the years. We recruited aggressively and hired some skilled journalists. We started doing some excellent investigative

---

reporting, exposing corruption and wrongdoing and winning state and national awards. We went from one of Gannett's worst newspapers to one of its best.

I tried to enjoy those times because I knew they probably wouldn't last. At successful mid-sized newspapers, it is often difficult to keep talented people because bigger newspapers will recruit them. After spending years building and then rebuilding our staff, I wasn't interested in doing it again. It was time to move on to a different challenge.

People sometimes cling to the past and try to avoid dealing with the present and the future. They're not being realistic. Situations change even if they don't want them to change.

That's why it is important to live in the present. Much has been written about how little time we spend in the present. We spend significant time dwelling on the past or focusing on the future. If we do that, we miss a lot of what's going on now.

People often don't take the time to celebrate their successes. They're already thinking about their next potential conquest. This is true especially in sales where a person will make goal one period but will already be worried about how difficult it will be to repeat that in the next period.

It's usually later in life when people realize they should have appreciated the good times more.

That happened to Roy Williams, the extremely successful basketball coach at the University of North Carolina. He had a scare with cancer that helped put his life in perspective.

He told then *USA Today* columnist Mike Lopresti that during that time he realized he should have taken more time to savor the national championships his teams had won. He recalled that in 2009, just 36 hours after the Tar Heels won the NCAA title, he was standing in a parking lot in Ames, Iowa, waiting to see a recruit.

It's unfortunate that it frequently takes an illness to put things into perspective.

Fortunately, surgery determined that both Williams' tumors were benign. He said that experience caused him to remember each day how blessed he is to be alive. He's trying to enjoy the journey more because a few years ago he feared that journey could end soon.

He said that experience caused him to remember each day how blessed he is to be alive. He's trying to enjoy the journey more because a few years ago he feared that journey could end soon.

Williams got a chance to once more enjoy the journey and the satisfaction that comes from winning it all. His Tar Heels won the men's national basketball championship in 2017, beating Gonzaga in the finals. The victory was especially sweet for Williams since his team got upset by Villanova the year before in the finals.

There's a great quote, author unknown: "If you worry about what might be, and wonder what might have been, you will ignore what is."

So if you have had a good day, enjoy that day. If you've had a good week, enjoy that week.

BOOM! BOOM!

Appreciate what you've got and that will certainly help you along the way.

Tip No. 28:

A Six-pack for Your Career

You're familiar with a six-pack of soda.

You're likely familiar with a six-pack of beer.

But how about a six-pack labeled "Career?"

Fortunately you've come to the right place. Here's what it means:

For those looking for a job, what if you did six things a week to help you in your search?

So what could they be? Here are some examples:

- o   Update your resume.
- o   Contact your references to let them know what you are pursuing.
- o   Network with people to let them know what you are seeking.
- o   Do research on potential companies.

- Go on LinkedIn to see if you know anyone at the companies you are considering.
- Clean up your social media profile.

You should easily be able to add other examples that you could do.

If you do six things a week or six things every other week, you will be putting yourself in a better position to get a job. There's also a satisfaction knowing at the end of the week that you are making concrete steps to potentially land that job.

Now you say, the six-pack for your Career works great if you are looking for a job. Could it possibly work if you already have a job and are looking for a better one either inside or outside your company? The answer is a resounding "Yes."

Here are some examples that you could do:

- Improve your skills so you will be qualified for a new job.
- Talk with your supervisor, letting him or her know about your interest in doing something else and always framing your comments on how it will benefit the company.
- Reach out to your network to let them know what you would like to pursue.

- Seek out people who already have the position you want, finding the best people at that job and finding out the skills that make them successful.
- Tailor your resume to showcase your skills that make you eligible for that new job.
- Find a mentor who takes an interest in you and can help you through the process.

Again, if you did six things a week or even in a month, you will be working your way to what you want. Remember, the person who should care the most about your career is you, so don't sit back and wait for another day or week. The time to start is now.

Then when people ask how you are doing in your job search, you can tell them proudly that you just finished off a six-pack. When they look aghast, you can say, "I just did a six- pack – a six-pack to benefit my career."

BOOM! BOOM!

How much is a six-pack of your career worth? Priceless.

YOUR BOOM! BOOM! TAKEAWAYS

_____

_____

_____

_____

_____

_____

_____

_____

_____

_____

_____

_____

_____

_____

_____

CHAPTER 5
SO YOU WANT
TO BE A MANAGER

Tip No. 29:

Think Before YOU Leap

Talented people in their particular professional field are occasionally encouraged to move into management. Often these people feel obligated to do so to "advance their career."

My advice: think carefully before making the leap.

There is no corollary between someone who is a successful sales representative and someone who is a successful sales manager. They take different skills and different traits. Someone who is an average sales rep could end up being an excellent sales manager. A consistently goal-achieving sales rep could struggle as a manager. The same is true for non-managers and managers in any field.

For most non-managers, their focus is on themselves. Their success or failure – as a sales rep, a reporter or a chemist – is pretty much controlled by them. They can be "me" focused. A manager's success or failure is controlled in part by the people they manage. If the team isn't successful, the manager won't be. They have to be "we" focused.

A manager often lives vicariously through his or her people. The manager may not be the person making the sale or writing the story. His or her people are doing that. A manager gains satisfaction knowing that the coaching that he or she provided helped in making the sale or writing the story.

It's a shame when people are pushed into management who really don't belong.

We had a talented advertising sales rep in Phoenix who consistently exceeded goal. She was energetic, creative and awesome with customers. She was perfect for what she did and loved her work.

She realized she would make a lousy manager. She was self-centered, focused on her part of the business and loved being on the front lines. She had no interest in coaching or managing others.

It would be a crime to make her a manager. But companies often come to the conclusion, "she's been successful in sales, let's make her a manager."

Companies should avoid developing an organizational culture where success is judged solely by those who want to go into management.

Companies need to embrace and reward the successful people who have no interest in management and stop trying to convince them to go into management.

A successful company is like an award-winning philharmonic. Not everyone can play the same instrument. They need people playing a variety of instruments. A company needs talented managers, but also talented non-managers.

For people who don't want to manage others, they should be embraced for the contributions they make to the organization.

BOOM! BOOM!

Not everyone is cut out to be a manager. But if you do have an interest, the following tips are for you.

Tip No. 30:
Seven Most Important Words

New managers often seem like they are carrying the proverbial weight of the world on their shoulders. They are letting their employees burden them with their problems. As the expression goes, they are allowing others to put monkeys on their back.

Don't allow people to do that.

There's one way to make sure that doesn't happen. When someone comes to you with a problem or concern and asks, "What should I do?" pause and then remember to say these seven powerful words:

"What do YOU think you should do?"

If people know that their manager is always going to give them the answer, they'll stop thinking on their own.

I've frequently heard people say: "I don't know why we are doing this but that's what the boss wanted."

Those people have washed their hands of the problem. They're not engaged in finding a solution.

By asking people, "What do YOU think you should do?" it forces them to have thought of a solution or a recommendation. They will soon learn that they just can't dump problems on you.

Young managers may want to show they're smart and that "they have all the answers." The better way is to find out what your employees are thinking.

By getting their thoughts, you can assess their thinking process.

- Do they have creative solutions?
- Do they think outside the box?
- Do they possess the necessary critical thinking skills that could make them promotable?

If their solutions are the ones you would have suggested, so much the better. They will be more eager to implement the solution because it was their idea, not one from their boss.

If you don't like their solutions, then ask them questions about how they arrived at that decision. Often by asking questions, people will realize the shortcomings of their decision.

Shortly after arriving in Rochester, I worked with an assistant sports editor who always rewrote the headlines that copy editors put on stories. One co-worker in frustration muttered after writing a headline, "What does it matter? He's just going to rewrite it anyway."

Instead of empowering his employees, the assistant sports editor was stifling them. If he had engaged his employees and worked with them on improving the headlines, he would have been more successful.

BOOM! BOOM!

Remember the secret of management: Getting employees to do what you want and having them think it's their idea.

Tip No. 31:

Your Words Carry Weight

Remember this axiom: in a chain of command, a conversation means more to a direct report than it does to the boss.

Let me explain: my first boss in Phoenix was president and publisher Sue Clark-Johnson. When we talked, I usually could remember almost every word of our conversation. I was likely to tell my wife. To Sue, it was likely a blip in her day. The conversation meant more to me than it did to her. Now, if her boss had called her, that's a different story.

That same day, I might have a conversation with an advertising manager or a sales rep. Afterward, I might not think of it again. It almost never would be something I'd tell my wife. But to that manager or sales rep, that's a conversation they might recount to others. The conversation meant more to them than it did to me.

That might seem cold hearted, but it is reality.

I remember getting an email from a community editor, profusely thanking me for giving him career advice. I felt like a goof. I couldn't remember precisely what I told him but obviously it made a big impact on him.

In conversations with employees, I always saw it as me talking. To them, they saw it as the position talking. The position you hold in an organization carries weight.

Once, after a sales rep had switched work areas, I walked by his desk. His desk usually was meticulous. This day everything was a mess. I kidded him about it and then never gave it another thought. Late in the day, I walked by again. He proudly wanted to show me that his desk was perfect. My offhanded comment he had taken seriously because as the boss, I had made it.

When first coming to Pensacola as managing editor, I worked with a deputy managing editor. After the first afternoon news meeting ran about 45 minutes, I had a casual conversation with her. I mentioned that those news meetings should last no more than 30 minutes unless there were extenuating circumstances. People needed to get back to work. I wasn't asking for it to be changed right then. I was talking out loud.

The next day, the executive editor needed to see me so I didn't make the afternoon meeting. Later, the deputy managing editor came up to me and eagerly said, "You would have been so proud. The meeting was over in less than 30 minutes."

I realized a valuable lesson: be careful what you tell people. You might be thinking you're talking out loud. They'll take it as an order.

Employees likely will respect you more as a manager if you are visible. Tom Sadvary, former HonorHealth CEO, warns new managers to avoid a "bunker" mentality.

"It is so easy to hide in your office answering phone calls and emails," he said. "To really understand what's going on in the organization you need to get out and walk around and talk with people."

Doing that helps you stay connected to the organization and enhances your credibility. It also helps you understand the challenges your team might be facing and provides you with the opportunity to engage workers in conversations about how the company might improve the operation. Remember: front-line people often have good ideas to make things work better.

Managers being visible is especially important when times are tough and when the organization could be dealing with issues such as greater competition, disappointing earnings or downsizing.

"This is when you really need to be with your team," he said.

BOOM! BOOM!

In business, people often don't see the person,
they see the position.

Tip No. 32:

Hiring the Right People is the Key

Your success or lack of success as a manager will likely come down to one major factor: how successful are you at hiring the right people and then providing them the work environment and the tools to succeed.

Great people can make even mediocre managers look great. Then again, if they spotted and recruited such great talent, how mediocre can those managers really be?

The best managers are those who surround themselves with talented people who help the company thrive. Too often, some managers are so insecure in their own abilities that they feel threatened by people who they fear could one day take their jobs. Those managers forget that if the company succeeds, those talented people could take their jobs because those managers could get promoted to even bigger jobs.

In Jim Collins' best-selling book, *Good to Great*, he details how the best managers make sure they hire the right people – or to

---

use his term – to get the right people on the bus. Then the bus is ready to hit the road on the path to greatness.

So how do you find the right people? You determine the skill sets that are needed. Then you look for people who are smart, passionate and eager to make a meaningful contribution.

The key is to hire a variety of people – not just carbon copies of yourself. The best companies embrace diversity, whether that is gender, racial or educational. In this dynamic global environment, companies need the perspectives that people from different life experiences can provide.

The big thing to remember in hiring is not to settle. Just because you have an opening, doesn't mean you have to fill it tomorrow. My biggest hiring mistakes came when deciding to settle on a candidate instead of continuing the search. Remember: it's much harder to get rid of someone once he or she is your employee.

Also, always be recruiting even if you don't have an opening. You never know when an opening will occur and you always need to be thinking ahead.

One of my favorite stories about hiring came from a former colleague, John Misner, then chief operating officer for Republic

Media and general manager of KPNX-TV. He recounted a conversation he had with a boss when John was a new manager. He called his boss to discuss terminating an employee that one of John's direct reports had hired less than a year prior. John's boss asked just one question about the soon-to-be-dismissed employee: "Was he bad when you hired him or did he get bad under your leadership?"

Ouch! John describes the question as an "MBA in 15 words" as it succinctly addresses a leader's responsibility to hire well and to lead well.

BOOM! BOOM!

If you do decide to pursue being a manager, just know this: hiring will either make or break you.

Tip No. 33:

Fatal Flaws as a Manager:

Here is some advice on things not to do if you want to succeed as a manager.

1) HERE'S HOW WE DID IT ...

Picture this scenario: you've been a successful manager at one of your company's properties. You've done so well that the company wants to promote you to a different location. You're eager for a new challenge and accept the promotion. You hustle off to your new location and start work.

Want a sure-fire way to turn off your new employees? Just start telling them about how you used to handle situations at your former job. "In (fill in the city), we used to do it this way." Then look around at their faces. They'll turn you off faster than you can turn off a light.

I once worked with an advertising director who moved from a smaller newspaper in Kansas City to a bigger newspaper in Phoenix. He was a nice guy. However, almost every time he mentioned a certain project or idea, he would preface it by saying that's what he did in Kansas City.

You should have seen the eye-rolling. People kept thinking, "What's so great about that place? We're better than that place."

This fatal error gets committed by new managers time after time. It's unbelievable. Don't let it happen to you.

Why does it matter where the idea came from? Just don't mention the city. Say, "Here's an idea we could try."

People will be more receptive if they know you're just not trying to replicate the same things you did in earlier positions.

2) "I NEED TO CHECK WITH MY BOSS"

One of the key traits a manager must have with his or her employees is credibility. Here's a way to avoid losing it.

See what I mean from these examples with Sarah as the employee, Jim as the manager and Margaret as Jim's boss:

Scenario 1:

Sarah: "Jim, what should we do with the Weber account? When I went to see them today they want a 50 percent credit on their recent ad because we ran the wrong address. Can we give them the 50 percent credit?"

Jim: "I don't know. Let me talk with Margaret about it and I'll get back with you."

Scenario 2:

Sarah: "Jim, I'm putting together the proposal for Rogers Furniture. Can we give them a 30 percent discount if they sign a 26-week contract?"

Jim: "Thirty percent, huh. That's a big discount. Let me run it by Margaret and I'll get back to you."

Scenario 3:

Sarah: "Jim, what are you going to do about Nicole? She promised me she would have the artwork I needed by this morning and now she called in sick. She's killing me. She's so irresponsible. I'm furious."

Jim: "Calm down, Sarah. Let me talk with Margaret about it."

What do you notice about these three decisions?

Jim can't make a decision. He's always checking with his boss, Margaret.

How do you think Sarah feels?

She's probably thinking, "Why am I bothering to tell Jim? I should go right to Margaret."

Managers who repeatedly say that they have to check with their boss are just emasculating themselves. They lose credibility with their employees every time they utter those words.

So how should Jim have handled the situations?

Scenario 1:

Sarah: "Jim, what should we do with the Weber account? When I went to see them today they want a 50 percent credit on their recent ad because we ran the wrong address. Can we give them the 50 percent credit?"

Jim: "Let me take a look at the ad. I'll get back with you."

Scenario 2:

Sarah: "Jim, I'm putting together the proposal for Rogers Furniture. Can we give them a 30 percent discount if they sign a 26-week contract?"

Jim: "Bring me your proposal so I can review it to see if it makes sense."

Scenario 3:

Sarah: "Jim, what are you going to do about Nicole? She promised me she would have the artwork I needed by this morning and now she called in sick. She's killing me. She's so irresponsible. I'm furious."

Jim: "Calm down, Sarah. Let me do some checking on the ad."

In each case, Jim might want to talk with his boss, Margaret, about the issue but Sarah doesn't need to know that.

Jim also might just want time alone to figure out the ramifications of each issue. Just because someone comes to Jim with a problem, doesn't mean he has to give that person a quick answer. If Jim needs time to think before giving Sarah an answer, he needs to take it.

Often times managers make mistakes when they make rash decisions. They might be preoccupied dealing with another issue and haven't considered the ramifications a quick decision about another issue might cause. They need to take their time unless it is truly an urgent issue.

BOOM! BOOM!

Avoid the fatal flaws and you'll be much
more successful as a manager.

YOUR BOOM! BOOM! TAKEAWAYS

_____

_____

_____

_____

_____

_____

_____

_____

_____

_____

_____

_____

_____

_____

_____

_____

CHAPTER 6
TAKING CONTROL

Tip No. 34:

Your Boss is Not Your Friend

That might seem strange – your boss is not your friend?

Simple answer: that's because your boss is your boss.

Now it's great to have a solid, professional relationship with your boss. That person can likely help you achieve your goals in an organization and help determine your success and possible advancement.

Still, it's always good to remember that he or she is your boss.

Too often, people who thought of their boss as their friend shared details that ultimately came back to harm them and their careers.

An acquaintance of mine shared a story about her relationship with her boss. She let it be known how happy she was at her job because her family lived in a neighboring city. She later felt her boss and the company weren't concerned about her leaving for another job so they didn't offer her promotions and salary

---

increases like someone whom the company feared might quit.

Some people share with their boss personal details about their life that would be better left unsaid. This can especially happen after hours when a group gets together. People get relaxed and start saying things they might regret later.

Remember just like in court: whatever you tell your boss, can and will be used against you.

If you need to share intimate details about your life, be judicious and a find a friend or confidant you can confide in who will keep your trust.

The same holds true for bosses. They can't get so close to their employees that it impacts their thinking and decision making.

"Maintaining the healthy work/professional relationship with employees is very important," one boss said. "It is my own human nature to connect with my employees on somewhat of a personal level. It's who I am to do that. But I can never let that cross the line where I don't feel comfortable giving them constructive feedback or having to give them a tough project. It's all about balance."

This boss also shared her thoughts on what she looks for in hiring.

"When I was in process of backfilling a position, I was having some struggles with the interview process," she said. "One of my friends (former co-workers) gave me some great advice. She said to look at what this position/candidate can do for you. Being in a higher-level position, this person needs to make your job easier, not harder. So I started to frame some of my questions with that in mind and it really helped me realize as an interviewer what I was looking for. So I guess advice on the flip side is for the interviewee to be prepared with how not only they are an asset to the company, but to their potential boss, team and the function in which they are interviewing for."

No matter how close a relationship you might have with your boss, sometimes a boss is going to have to make hard decisions. When the company is struggling, for example, the boss might have to lay you off. Your friendship is likely not going to save you.

Also, think twice before informing your boss about possible successes that have yet to occur. An advertising colleague told his boss about a $100,000 contract a new advertiser was likely going to sign. The boss – similar to all bosses – skipped over the key word "likely." In the boss' mind it was already a done deal. When the sales representative came back later with a contract from a new advertiser for $50,000, the boss didn't congratulate him on landing a new advertiser. He asked, "What happened to the other $50,000?

If the sales representative needed to tell somebody, he should have told a friend.

What should have the sales rep done? He should have waited until he had a signed agreement with the new advertiser. Then he would have looked like a hero with his boss.

Having a supportive boss is wonderful. Having someone who inspires and elevates your performance is wonderful. Having someone who has the right temperament for the job is wonderful.

What's not wonderful is if you forget who that person is. That's your boss.

BOOM! BOOM!

Be careful what you share with your boss.
He or she is your boss for a reason.

Tip No. 35:

Your Boss Isn't a Mind Reader
And Neither are YOU!

Here's a guarantee: at least once in your business career you will hear a colleague say, "I don't know why I wasn't considered for that promotion? I've got more skills than the person who got promoted. I'm doing great work. How come I'm not getting recognized?"

There's often a simple reason – the person never spoke up about showing interest in that promotion.

Too often, people think that their bosses are mind readers – that they know exactly what the employees' goals are and what jobs they desire.

It's almost as if people expect, like out of medieval times, that the boss will come down and lay a sword on the employee's shoulder and say, "I knight you the new vice president of sales." Then the employee would mount his or her horse and ride off to the new job.

News flash: bosses aren't mind readers. They won't know what you want out of your career unless you tell them.

That's why it is important to discuss with them your aspirations and how you would like to see your career progress.

Keep in mind; you need to present it as how – with additional responsibilities – you can be more valuable to the company. In the end, your boss and your company are more interested in what's in it for them, than what's in it for you.

People who get ahead are often people who take on challenging assignments, obtain additional training and/or education and stay committed to the organization. They're people who can navigate the occasional land mines of office politics. They're people who have developed a network of allies within the company.

Sometlmes you need to force the issue. I speak from experience.

Less than one year after arriving as a sports reporter/copy editor at the Times-Union, our assistant sports editor took another job at the newspaper. Since none of the other staffers – all older than me – had an interest in the position, I stepped in and started to fill the void.

I worked extra hours and took on a bunch of additional duties. Occasionally my sports editor would encourage me to put in overtime but I never did. I wanted to show that I was a hard worker willing to do all that I could to get promoted.

However, the managing editor was reluctant to promote me. I was just 23 and this was a significant job for someone so young. I remember one day going to lunch with her and providing reasons why she should promote me. Still no promotion.

In October, my sports editor and his wife went on vacation to Maine, leaving me in charge. A freak early snowstorm hit there and he got delayed in returning home. During that time I had to put together the special annual hockey preview section in addition to all the other duties.

When he got back, he said this is ridiculous, that this time he was definitely putting in overtime for me.

A week later I got promoted. Now as a salaried employee, I was no longer eligible for overtime. I always kicked myself that if I had allowed my boss to put in overtime six months earlier, I might have gotten promoted sooner.

One of the best habits to get into is keeping a detailed record of your accomplishments.

This will prove invaluable when having to write a self evaluation.

I'm often amazed at how the mind works. You will work on a major project that consumes lots of time and effort. You'll think, "There's no way I'll forget about this."

Nine months later, you're doing your self evaluation and you forget to mention it because you've been involved in many other projects and events since then.

That's why it is up to you to keep good notes.

A great way to do that is to create a computer folder where you type in these accomplishments as the year goes on. If it's something tangible, have a file in your desk where you can put it.

Spending time to do a detailed self evaluation will also help your boss when he or she writes your review. Don't expect them to remember all the great things you have done. Your boss has more than you to worry about. When he or she gets around to writing your review, they are often stressed for time, so the easier you can make it for them, the better it is for you.

As a manager, the same idea applies. Create files on each of your employees and write notes about accomplishments, failures or other events that take place.

If a manager doesn't, he or she often will forget about how the employee 10 months ago botched a project.

Being disciplined and taking a few moments each week to note the important things that happened will save you lots of frustration later.

Many companies, during the yearly evaluations, seek out the career interests and goals of employees. That's well and good, but if you are serious about moving ahead, these conversations need to happen more regularly.

Seeking out feedback from your boss is key, not only on your current job performance but on your short-term and long-term goals. That way there should be no surprises on how your boss thinks you are performing. That way you should have an idea that if a possible promotion came up, whether you would be considered.

BOOM! BOOM!

The person who your career means most to is you. Putting yourself in the position to get what you want is up to you. If you wait to get knighted, it could be a long night.

Tip No. 36:

Don't Love the Company, the Company Can't Love You Back

Eastman Kodak dominated Rochester, N.Y., for decades. The film giant's corporate headquarters were there and more than 60,000 people at one time worked for the company there.

Being employed at Kodak was like having a job for life. Often generations of families worked there. The company had a long-deserved reputation of taking care of its employees and, in turn, employees felt extremely loyal to Kodak. Many workers couldn't conceive working elsewhere.

If you lived in Rochester and didn't work at Kodak, you probably worked at Xerox, which had a huge operation, or at Bausch + Lomb, which produced RayBan sunglasses.

These companies were pillars of Rochester's employment base and its economy.

Times changed. All three companies eventually struggled as competition and new technologies disrupted their businesses. They often were slow to adjust.

While earning my MBA, one of my management professors was Don Zrebiec, at the time a vice president for human resources at Xerox. He said something in class in 1990 that still resonates with me today:

"Don't love the company, the company can't love you back."

More than 20 years later, I asked him about the message he was trying to convey to his students:

"A huge 'sea change' started in the 1980's in U.S. industry that affected all employees but these same employees did not see it coming, maybe because they didn't understand the nature of the change or maybe because they did not want to see it," Zrebiec said. "Layoffs began in the 80's in industries and companies that never had seen layoffs driven by lower profit numbers that in many cases were caused by foreign competition.

"In the early 90's, this 'sea change' became official when IBM and Kodak both fired their CEOs. This was extremely significant because both companies prided themselves on two things: an almost guarantee of lifetime employment and a strict policy of promotion from within. IBM's CEO John Akers was a product of a 30-year career all with IBM and Kay Whitmore followed the same path at Kodak. In fact, IBM had a written policy of continued employment that was the pride of U.S. industry.

"Not only did these two titans get fired but they were replaced with people not only from outside the company but from outside of their core industries. AT&T, DuPont and Xerox as well as a number of admired Fortune Top 50 companies had similar policies."

Employees were now on their own, Zrebiec said, but most did not see it coming or know that it had arrived.

"Employees with these large companies still felt they had a special relationship and although they might have heard rumors of layoffs somewhere within their companies, they continued with the attitude that it wouldn't and couldn't happen to them," he said. "And when it finally did, they were devastated. Their sense of identity, their relationship with their families, and their status in the community were shaken to the core.

"My statement 'don't love the company, the company can't love you back' was an attempt to wake employees to the new reality, to the dramatically changed environments they were now part of," Zrebiec said. "It was attempting to emphasize that their relationship with their company was an economic one and could and probably would be terminated any time those economics changed."

Zrebiec said he derived that statement from an interview he was having with a vice president at Xerox.

"I knew he was in trouble and he would not accept the fact that his continued employment was on shaky ground," Zrebiec said. "When he first entered my office, he emotionally stated that he loved this place. As soon as he said this, I asked him to leave and return when he was able to have a more objective discussion with me about his options.

"He came back two days later and said that after a great deal of thought, he knew why I dismissed him from the first discussion. Incidentally, he survived that 'crisis' and was pretty successful until a friend of his from Xerox became a senior VP at Kodak and he quit Xerox and went there. He learned his lesson well."

Zrebiec sees parallels to the recent transformation in the U.S. auto industry where workers who thought they had union-protected jobs for life have gotten a rude awakening.

"The other admonition I gave to employees and students was to keep a well-written resume up to date and not be afraid to use it," he said. "Some people, though, still not accepting the change in the employment 'contract' in U.S. industry, complained that keeping an updated resume and sending it out for a better opportunity was an act of disloyalty to their current employer."

That's why one of Zrebiec's favorite quotes comes from former star baseball pitcher Don Sutton: "I am the most loyal ballplayer that money can buy."

Zrebiec feels that today's employees are starting to accept the new reality.

"I have a brother-in-law with four children, two in college and he has had five jobs in the last 10 years. He is doing well and would not hesitate to pursue a sixth job if it met his needs. His attitude is, 'I am as loyal to the company I work for as they are to me.'"

BOOM! BOOM!

It's great to have loyalty to your company,
just don't have blind loyalty.

Tip No. 37:

It's Not About Love, It's About Value

Here's a different view on the previous tip about not loving the company because the company can't love you back. How about: "A company doesn't need to love you but it does need to value you."

That perspective comes from Jim Malvaso, who had an extremely successful career culminating with him being chairman and CEO of the Raymond Corporation, a leading manufacturer of forklift trucks and pallet jacks, and president & CEO of Toyota Material Handling North America. He also happens to be my brother-in-law.

He sees the relationship between a company and its employees as a partnership.

"It's not about like or love, it's a value relationship," Malvaso said. "All companies, regardless of sectors, invest in assets that they believe will bring value to their customers and owners alike. These may be hard assets, soft assets, intellectual assets or human assets. The latter often times being the most complex, yet most valuable. The underlying strategy is to leverage these assets better than anyone else to yield the most value. The human asset expects, and yes, deserves value in return for their contributions to the company's success."

Employees accomplish that by being in sync with the company's goals.

"Embracing and understanding a company's strategy and using your talents to help the company achieve that strategy increases your value to the company," he said. "That is rewarded in many ways, financial, position, title, responsibility, etc. As you enter into a relationship with an employer, look for the mutual opportunities to provide each other value."

Ultimately it comes down to how much value you provide the company and how much value the company is providing you.

As many organizations flatten their organizational structures, there will be plenty of opportunities for those who seize them to enhance their value. This often requires taking on more responsibilities or learning additional skills. Being recognized as someone who is flexible and willing to step up when the need arises will enhance your value.

A prime example of that is the newspaper business.

Before, a successful measurement of a reporter was how skilled he or she was at writing for the daily newspaper. With the decline of newspaper readership, that's no longer the case. A reporter now needs many skills. He or she needs to know how to write for the newspaper's website, how to take and edit pictures and video, how to generate content and followers for the company's social media accounts and much more. A reporter who only has skills to write for the daily newspaper is not as valued as before.

The value proposition is changing dramatically in many industries especially because of technology. Look at just some other industries/businesses that have been greatly impacted:

Travel: Before people used to depend on travel agents to book trips. Now many people do it themselves online.

Bookstores: Before people used to actually go into physical stores to search for and buy books. Now many people buy books online. Some don't end up buying physical copies of books but digital ones they can read on their tablets.

Financial services: Before people used a broker to buy stocks and bonds. Now many people do their own trading online.

Imagine the disruption that driverless cars and trucks will

cause and the people and businesses that will be hugely impacted. Your ability to adapt to these changing times is essential because your value to a company today could be far less in the future if your skill sets don't keep up.

"The more you actually achieve and the more value you provide will help you stand out and be recognized as someone the company will be willing to invest in," Malvaso said.

He offers these other perspectives:

- **Control what you can to the utmost for there are many things outside of your control that you will need the time and resources to respond to.** Malvaso remembers meeting with his vice president of marketing about the company's declining market share. The vice president started to complain about the recession that was currently occurring in the nation. He stopped the VP and said, "When you fix the economy, let me know." The point: the VP had no control over the national economy. The VP did have control over his company's marketing efforts. For example, was the VP allocating the company's marketing resources in the most effective way to generate business? Remember: your boss doesn't want to hear excuses, he or she wants to hear ideas on how you can turn problems into opportunities.

- Don't shy away from setting aggressive but attainable goals in both your personal and professional life. "Setting a high bar and missing it by a little is better than setting a low bar and exceeding it by a lot." When people set a low bar they often lack incentive to push themselves.

- Be willing to take risks but do it smartly. Develop a list of "what ifs" so if one plan doesn't work out, you have contingency plans in mind. That way you aren't taking risks haphazardly and you are prepared to adjust course quickly.

- Don't subscribe to the "stupid customer theory." Some sales people and business leaders think they are smarter than the customer. That can often be fatal in landing or keeping customers. Know your customer, whether internal or external. There are often reasons why customers may not embrace a solution that may seem obvious to you. Helping them solve their real problems will enable you to become their most valuable asset that is not on their balance sheet. This is essential to having a long lasting relationship.

He provides this final thought on leadership. "A mark of a good leader is not how well people follow but how many leaders they create."

Finally, there are two certainties in business:

1) **Change will continue at a rapid pace.** We are no where close to the end of the technological revolution. More and more jobs people used to handle will be taken over by automation. That's why it is so important to keep refining and updating your skills. The person who is responsible for doing that is you. Your company might help you but you better be the one taking the lead.

2) **Your success in your career will be an ongoing challenge.** The value you bring to the company today could be less in the future if you don't keep up. There are plenty of workers out there who once were at the top of their field who are no longer on top because they didn't stay current and refine their skills. Don't let that happen to you.

BOOM! BOOM!

In business as in life, it all comes down to the value
you bring to the relationship and how much value
the relationship brings to you.

Tip No. 38:
It Can't Happen to Me. Wanna Bet?

Some people think their careers are bullet proof. They believe they will always have success and that their career will be one giant shot straight up like a rocket.

These people see their colleagues or peers fail or experience disappointments but it seemingly doesn't have an impact on them. It's almost like people who don't want to look at a car crash on the side of the road.

Their attitude is: "It can't happen to me."

Wanna bet? Just wait and see.

Sorry to burst any balloons, but bad things can happen to good people. You can get into bad situations that aren't of your doing. You can and often will make mistakes of your own doing.

The mark of resiliency in a person is not whether he or she gets knocked down; it's how a person gets back up. That's going to determine one's overall success.

Disappointments in your career are bound to happen. As Al Neuharth remarked, failure can be embraced if you learn from it. How you handle disappointments and failure is the key.

As former world heavyweight champion Mike Tyson said: "Everyone has a plan 'till they get punched in the mouth."

I was always amazed at watching people in their careers in my 35 years with Gannett. Some people's careers were like an elevator. They went up and down. Those who were resilient hung in there during the tough times and got back to the top.

That's why it is important to have a strong core and belief in yourself. There will never be a shortage of co-workers and bosses who will love you when you succeed. Your true co-workers and bosses are the ones who will support you when you're down.

BOOM! BOOM!

Take it from legendary football coach Vince Lombardi: "The real glory is being knocked to your knees and then coming back. That's real glory. That's the essence of it."

Tip No. 39:

Follow Your Dream?

Amir Raza, mentioned in the introduction, and I discussed many topics during those late-afternoon conversations in my office. As we got to know each other better, he started sharing more about what he really wanted to do.

Amir had graduated from Indiana University in 2005. He had worked on his college newspaper selling advertising and eventually overseeing the advertising department. He attended a national conference where newspapers seek promising college sales people and was highly recruited. *The Chicago Tribune* and *Indianapolis Star* wanted him but he decided to take a risk and move to Phoenix and join *The Arizona Republic* advertising sales team. This did not go over well with his parents who wanted him closer to his home in Fort Wayne, Ind.

He joined the sales team in the Scottsdale office and was successful from the start. He has an engaging personality which helped him in going out and developing relationships with current and prospective clients. He consistently exceeded his sales goals.

Amir wanted more. He wanted to get into management. Within two years, he got that chance. *The Arizona Republic* was concerned about losing him so we created a hybrid position where he would manage a couple sales representatives and still have his own clients. This would give Amir valuable experience as a manager and allow us to groom him for bigger management roles. Amir appreciated the opportunity and soaked up any tips he could get from his sales manager, other advertising managers and me.

Still, Amir wasn't fulfilled. We began to talk about his days at Indiana where he worked on the college TV station as a reporter and anchor. The more we talked, the more he confided in me. Amir really wanted to get into broadcasting.

His desire seemed so eerily familiar. I, too, had wanted to get into broadcasting – as a sports TV announcer.

I had done some sports on TV. While a senior in high school – and while working part time as a sports reporter for *The Star-Gazette* in Elmira, N.Y. – I got a chance to fill in and do sports for the half-hour local news on TelePrompTer, the local cable company. This was about as basic a TV operation as there could be. There were no teleprompters – there was hardly a set – and who knows how many people even watched, but still it was TV.

The TelePrompTer station manager offered me a job the summer after graduating from high school. For a brief time I contemplated doing that and attending Elmira College but decided it was better to leave home to go to college.

At St. Bonaventure University, I did a little work on the campus radio station but was so involved with the campus newspaper, eventually becoming editor, that I didn't have time to do more.

In Rochester, in the early 1980s while sports editor of the *Times-Union*, the broadcast bug began to bite. I had gotten to know the local TV sports anchors while out covering events. Simeon Smith, the popular sports anchor at the ABC affiliate, allowed me to come in to cut an audition tape. I put together my own 4-minute sports package, including narrating the highlights.

Simeon and I critiqued the tape. It was rough but he thought I had potential. Then he offered the straight scoop. He said that if I was really serious about doing TV sports broadcasting, I would have to move to a small market, learn the craft, and then try to move up from there.

After lots of contemplation, I realized that didn't appeal to me. I didn't want to give up a great job that paid well and a community I enjoyed living in to move to a small town and start over.

I shared those reflections with Amir, something I had rarely shared with anyone.

I told Amir that if he was serious about going into broadcasting, he needed to do it now. The longer he waited, the more entrenched he would get. As a single guy – only having to take care of himself – he could pick up and move.

To Amir's credit, he decided to follow his dream. He started researching what it would take to become a TV reporter. He realized that in order to apply for a job – besides the usual stuff such as a resume – he needed an up-to-date demo tape, not one from college. He did a Google search to look for companies that could produce a professional audition tape. He found one in Augusta, Ga., called Talent Tapes. He learned that it would cost about $2,000 to create the tape plus the cost to fly to and stay in Georgia.

"This was the moment of truth," Amir now recalls. "I was going to have to pay $3,000 of my own hard-earned money to get a tape with no assurance that I would even get a TV job."

Amir and I talked about that.

"You sat me down and told me, 'If you're serious, this is what you've got to do,'" Amir said.

The audition tape was impressive – especially considering he had limited broadcasting experience. I set up a meeting so he could share it with the news director at the NBC affiliate in Phoenix. The news director told Amir that he should stay at *The Arizona Republic*, continue selling advertising and enroll at Arizona State University to take broadcasting classes.

That didn't sit well with Amir. He wanted to get into broadcasting now. He was willing to give up his sales management position at the Republic, his love for the Valley of the Sun and his many close friends to pursue his dream.

Amir's father was not happy.

"I don't understand it," he told Amir. "You've got a good job, a good career, you work for a stable company and you own your own house. The economy is really bad and you're thinking of giving all that up for a job in a field you don't even know. I don't approve of it."

Amir's response: "I'm 29. I don't have a wife or kids. If I'm ever going to take the risk, now is the time."

After an exhaustive search trying to find a TV station willing to give a broadcasting novice a chance, he landed a reporting position in December 2011 at WVVA, the NBC affiliate in

Bluefield, W.Va., located in the Appalachian Mountains. His starting salary: $21,000 a year or more than four times less than what he made at *The Arizona Republic.*

Still, it was a TV job and Amir wanted to try TV. He became the station's one-person bureau in Beckley, W.Va., 50 miles from Bluefield. As Amir jokes, he likely became the only Pakistani in southern West Virginia.

Learning the TV business from the bottom up was a challenge, especially since Amir was working by himself.

"When you're a one-man band, you're doing it all," he said. "I had to write, edit and shoot my own stories."

That meant lugging all the equipment along even when it was 20 degrees and snowing – a far cry from the warm winter weather in Arizona.

"There definitely were times when I wondered what the hell I was doing," he said.

The lowest point came when some friends invited him to see a new Batman movie.

"I couldn't even afford the $8.50 for the ticket," he said. "Two or three years before, I was going out with a work colleague to a sushi restaurant in Scottsdale and dropping $40 to $45 for lunch. Fast forward and now I couldn't even afford to go see a Batman movie I was dying to see."

Still Amir persevered.

"I told myself that I had to commit myself to this for at least a year," he said. "Then I could reassess. If you're not going to do that, you shouldn't even do it at all."

Amir never needed to reassess. He continued to grow and improve. And nine months after starting in Beckley, he got a big break. WSJV, the Fox affiliate in South Bend, Ind., hired him as a morning news reporter and fill-in anchor. Even though he had signed a two-year contract in Bluefield, he got to move to South Bend – home of the University of Notre Dame – since both stations are owned by Quincy Newspapers media group.

For Amir, he jumped from the 156th largest TV market to the 97th largest, according to Nielsen, an impressive leap for someone who had been in TV all of nine months.

In a couple years, Amir jumped up again. He moved to Grand Rapids, Mich., the nation's 40th largest TV market, where he is now the weekend news anchor and weekday reporter. He loves his job and doesn't miss selling newspaper advertising.

Amir has advice for people who are just graduating, just out of school or considering a career change.

"When you're young and not tied down, that's the time to take risks," he said. "Too often young people are told to take the safe path. What we should be telling them is to take the risk. Even if they fail at it, that's OK. The life experience from a failure could be more valuable down the road."

BOOM! BOOM!

Amir elected to follow his dream. If you have a real passion for something, are you willing to follow your dream?

Tip No. 40:

A Trapeze Artist

The rumors started toward the end of 2011. Gannett, my parent company, was planning to offer an early retirement program in the first quarter of 2012.

To say that my ears perked up like a dog sensing his supper would be an understatement. This could be a great opportunity for me.

I loved my work as vice president of *The Arizona Republic's* 18 community editions. I enjoyed my wide-ranging responsibilities including the opportunity to represent the company throughout the communities we served.

For years, though, I had contemplated retiring from Gannett before age 65. I never got excited about birthdays, especially after turning 40. But I certainly did as my 55th birthday approached because I knew I could then leave at any time and take my retirement benefits.

I knew there was much more that I wanted to do in life: start my own media consulting company, do pro bono communications work helping non-profits and to write this book.

A former *USA Today* employee had started the *Gannett Blog*, an independent journal about the company. This blog was a constant source of irritation for the company. On it was a lot of rampant speculation, but occasionally there were reports about people, issues or events that actually came true. I started checking it more often late at night or on weekends to see if there were any more details about the possible early retirement program.

As weeks rolled on, more details began to emerge and by early January more specific information started to come out: eligible employees would need to be at least 56 years old with at least 20 years of service with the company. Fifty six, not 55, that seemed curious for the starting age. I had assumed the cut-off age would be 55. Still, I had just turned 56 so that wasn't a problem. I easily had the years of service so I could be eligible.

I remember reading that on a Sunday afternoon and walking out of my office at home to tell my wife. This no longer appeared like idle speculation. The person feeding the blog seemed to have inside information. I needed to clue my wife in because if this early retirement option ever became reality, I wanted to seriously consider it. As always, my wife was extremely supportive.

Now the waiting game began. Each week I would go to my operating committee meeting thinking that this might be the time that my publisher, John Zidich, announced what the company planned. Weeks went by with no mention of an early retirement initiative.

Finally, more than a month later, the publisher announced the voluntary Early Retirement Opportunity Program (EROP). The specifics were just as the blog reported. The next day, eligible employees throughout the company would be notified and would have 45 days to decide since Gannett had to follow government guidelines.

Sure enough, the next day Zidich called me in and told me that I was eligible.

The company's offer to eligible employees was generous. In the Q&A provided, the company made that extremely clear saying "these offers are made very infrequently" and that this is "much more generous than the normal severance and/or transitional pay plan that we have provided in the past, which explains why they are offered only rarely."

In other words, if you are considering getting off the island, this ship is about to sail and don't expect a more luxurious ship to come take you away later.

To use a basketball term, the ball was now in my court. Now that I had the opportunity, would I pull the trigger and actually leave the company that I first joined as a part-time sports clerk in high school?

A few days later, I had lunch with a friend and what she said put it all in perspective for me. Her name is Donna Davis and she was getting ready to leave her position as chief executive officer of the Arizona Small Business Association. I told her about my opportunity and here is what she said:

"You need to see your life as a trapeze artist. A trapeze artist needs to release one bar to grab another. Are you willing to release the bar you're holding on to?"

Talk about profound words.

Those words stuck with me as I decided what to do. Was I willing to release the only bar I knew to grab on to a bar that I didn't know where it might lead me?

A few weeks later, my wife and I got together with her cousin and her husband. In telling him about my opportunity, he shared with me some insight that hit home: "If you turn this down, how are you going to feel in three months?" I knew that answer: I'd be bummed because I didn't grab the golden opportunity in front of me.

A couple weeks later, as the 45-day window to decide began to close, it was time to tell my boss. I felt extremely loyal to John Zidich. He had hired me 10 years ago and it had been a pleasure to work with him. He had helped make these years some of the most satisfying in my career.

Still I knew what I needed to do. He wanted me to stay but I felt it was time to leave.

It was finally time to release the bar.

BOOM! BOOM!

The transition between letting go of one bar and grabbing the new bar is often where the greatest growth and transformation occur. Donna warns, though, it's typically not comfortable.

YOUR BOOM! BOOM! TAKEAWAYS

_____

_____

_____

_____

_____

_____

_____

_____

_____

_____

_____

_____

_____

_____

CHAPTER 7
FINALLY

Reflection:

"Which One are YOU?"

Phil Currie, former senior vice president/news for Gannett, shared this poem with my class during a Senior Editor Management Development Program. He didn't know the author. The words are so powerful that I made a copy, put the poem in a frame and kept it in my office.

In closing, I ask: **WHICH ONE ARE YOU?**

I watched them tearing a building down,
A gang of men in a busy town.
With a ho-heave-ho and a lusty yell,
They swung a beam and the sidewall fell.

I asked the foreman, "Are these men skilled
And the kind you would hire if you had to build?"
He gave a laugh and said, "No indeed,
Just common labor is all I need.
I can easily wreck in a day or two
What other builders have taken a year to do."

I thought to myself as I went my way,

"Which of these roles have I tried to play?

Am I a builder that works with care

Measuring life by the rule and square?

Am I shaping my deeds to a well-made plan,

Patiently doing the best I can?

Or am I a wrecker who walks the town,

Content with the labor of tearing down?"

YOUR BOOM! BOOM! TAKEAWAYS

_____

_____

_____

_____

_____

_____

_____

_____

_____

_____

_____

_____

_____

KEEP THE CONVERSATION GOING

Hopefully you found useful the tips in *Make Your Career Go BOOM! Not Bust.* As mentioned in the introduction, I'm not so presumptuous to think these insights are all that you will need. My hope is that some of my experiences might help you have a successful and meaningful career.

Let's keep the conversation going. Please visit the Web site www.makeyourcareergoboom.com to share your own thoughts and your own BOOM! BOOM! tips. This way others can benefit from your knowledge and your experiences.

Please also check out our Facebook page, **@makeyourcareergoboom** and follow us on Twitter **@makeyourcareergoboom**. Also feel free to write us at *makeyourcareergoboom@gmail.com*

That's one way we can help "Pay It Forward."

ABOUT THE AUTHOR

Michael Ryan is an award-winning journalist with 35 years of media experience. He recently was a vice president of *The Arizona Republic* in Phoenix, overseeing as general manager all 18 community newspapers. He came from the *Pensacola (FL) News Journal* where he was managing editor and community newspaper publisher. Before that, he worked at *The Times-Union* in Rochester, N.Y., as sports editor, news editor and assistant managing editor. He also wrote a syndicated sports television column for Gannett News Service and occasionally for *USA Today*. He currently is president and CEO of Ryan Media Consultants, a full-service strategic communications and marketing company.

WHAT THEY ARE SAYING ABOUT MAKE YOUR CAREER GO BOOM! NOT BUST!

Ken Blanchard, co-author, The New One Minute Manager; co-editor, Servant Leadership In Action:

"I love Mike Ryan's book. It contains such down-to-earth career advice that I'm giving it to my four grandchildren in their 20s. The book has not only great career advice but, to me, wonderful advice for being a caring and loving human being. Don't miss it! This is one of the best self-help books I have read."

Jim Nantz, lead announcer at CBS Sports:

"A must read for college graduates and those new to the business world. This book is filled with practical and real-world advice rarely taught in school. The lessons shared such as Mike's Tips for Success could make a big difference in your ability to succeed in life and the workplace."

Rita Davenport, internationally known motivational speaker, author, entrepreneur:

"I travel the world asking people 'what is the unique gift you are meant to share?' Mike's gift is this book because he wants to see you have a successful, satisfying and meaningful career. Follow his tips learned from his years in business and you will be well on your way."

Joe Scarborough, host, Morning Joe, MSNBC:

"Here's something conservatives and liberals can agree on: Mike Ryan has given all Americans great advice in this book. As a father with two young adult sons, the guidance he offers will be of great help in their budding careers."

ISBN 978-0-9889488-3-9

US$14.99

CPSIA information can be obtained
at www.ICGtesting.com
Printed in the USA
FSHW020508031019
62646FS

9 781729 501399